BREAK
100
IN 21 DAYS

BREAK 100 IN 21 DAYS

A How-To Guide for the Weekend Golfer

BY WALTER OSTROSKE
PGA Teaching Pro

and JOHN DEVANEY

Photography by Aime La Montagne

A Perigee Book

Perigee Books
are published by
The Putnam Publishing Group
200 Madison Avenue
New York, NY 10016

Library of Congress Cataloging-in-Publication Data

Ostroske, Walter.
    Break 100 in 21 days: a how-to guide for the weekend golfer/by
    Walter Ostroske and John Devaney; photography by Aime La
    Montagne; designed by James McGuire.
        p.   cm.
    ISBN 0-399-51600-X
    1. Golf.   I. Devaney, John.   II. Title.   III. Title: Break one
    hundred in twenty-one days.
    GV965.O57   1990   89-29107 CIP
    796.352′3—dc20

Cover design © 1990 by Richard Rossiter
Cover photograph © 1990 by Aime La Montagne

Printed in the United States of America
20 19 18 17 16 15 14 13 12 11

This book has been printed on acid-free paper.

∞

Contents

At the Pro Shop: Say Hello to the 90s   9

Day 1: The Upper Gear: Grip, Stance, and the Three-Phase Swing   11

Day 2: The Lower Gear: The Feet, Knees, and Hips Coil or Pivot   21

Day 3: The Connecting Rod   29

Day 4: Think P-A-C-E, Think W-I-D-E   35

Day 5: Light Fire to the Clubhead   40

Day 6: The Swing's Sweet 16 Fundamentals   45

Day 7: The Pitch-and-Run: Your Best Way to Shave Strokes from a 100-Plus Score   48

Day 8: Putting: Your Next Best Way to Shave Strokes   53

Day 9: Blasting Out of Sand: It's One-Two Easy   60

Day 10: Hitting Off the Tee: A Game of Contradictions   67

Day 11: Fairway Woods: Remember Who's Boss—It's the Upper Gear!   72

Day 12: Long Irons: The Clubhead Leads the Parade   77

Day 13: Middle Irons: The Confidence Builders   84

Day 14: The Short Irons: Your Scoring Clubs   88

Day 15: Reading the Green: The Key to
Sinking Second Putts   94

Day 16: Coming Back From Trouble—In Only
One Stroke!   99

Day 17: Club Selection and Course Strategy:
Let One Stroke Do the Work of Two!   106

Day 18: Playing the Par 3s: Making the Most
Demanding Shot a Comfort Shot   110

Day 19: Playing the Par 4s: Why Misfortune
Need Not Cost You "Par"   113

Day 20: Playing the Par 5s: Where You Can
Be the Equal of the Long Hitters   116

Day 21: How the Rules Can Save You Strokes   120

The Day You Break 100   124

To Georgette, for making
life and golf what they
are—just great.

And to the members of
The Hempstead Golf and
Country Club for the years
of experience that became
the pages of this book.
—W.O.

My thanks to the officers, members,
and staff of the Hempstead Golf and
Country Club, where all the photos for
this book were made. Their cooperation and
kindness was invaluable, and the spectacular
beauty of their course is one I will
remember.
—J.D.

Walter Ostroske: Remember "Up, down, and through"—the three basic phases of the golf swing.

At the Pro Shop: Say Hello to the 90s

You have never broken 100. Your friends break 100. They shoot in the 80s and 90s. You have asked yourself, "Why can't I shoot the scores that they shoot? Why can't I play this game without embarrassing myself?"

As a PGA teaching pro for more than 20 years and as head pro at the Hempstead Golf and Country Club in Hempstead, New York, I have taught thousands of golfers—men and women, beginners as well as those who have played for years—how to break 100.

Using super-fast techniques, I have taught golfers who play only on weekends. Actually, 90 percent of the 21 million who play golf in the United States today are weekend golfers. The typical one will say to me, "Look, Walter. I play only ten, fifteen, or twenty times a year, mostly on Saturdays or Sundays. I have little time for practice. But I want to come in with scores like those of my friends, the ones who play two and three times a week."

More often than not, I have seen the scores of weekend golfers drop from 110 to 95, 90, and even into the low 80s. What I have done for them is what I propose to do for you.

The key to shooting below 100 is learning a swing that is the same swing for all clubs and for 99 percent of all shots. I have taught weekenders how to break 100 in three weeks— 21 days—by teaching them the two basics of this golf swing:

1) The swing is simple—up, down, through.

2) You swing at the ball. You don't hit at the ball. It is a golf swing, not a golf hit.

Give me 21 days, one day for each of the 21 lessons in this

book. During these lessons, I will cover the basic swing, grip, and stance; hitting long and short irons; hitting off the tee; pitching to the green within fifty yards; putting, reading greens; and hitting trouble shots out of the rough, sand, and trees. On days 18, 19, and 20, we'll play three holes: par 3, par 4, and par 5. Finally, on day 21, I'll show you how the rules can save you strokes.

I'll also need a half hour a day of your time for practicing on your own. You can practice on a range if one happens to be nearby. But you can practice most of these lessons in the backyard, a nearby vacant lot, even in your home. Our first lesson, for example, tells you how to grip the club properly, and you can grip a club most anywhere and at any time when your hands are free.

If you are a reasonably coordinated person—if you can hit a softball in a game at a picnic, or toss a basketball through a hoop at least once in ten tries—then you can break 100 after these 21 days of lessons.

Golf doesn't have to be as difficult a game as some books would make it out to be. Recently, I met an art director of a magazine who had been playing golf for more than 20 years and had yet to break 100.

"Len," I said to him, "this is a game where you pick up the club, bring it down and through. Up, down, through. That's all there is to a golf swing. Phase One, Phase Two, Phase Three. Up, down, through."

Len went out onto a course and reminded himself before and during each swing: "Up, down, through." Len now shoots in the 90s. These 21 days of lessons can do the same for you.

DAY 1

The Upper Gear: Grip, Stance, and the Three-Phase Swing

How you grip the club will determine how you impact the ball. The reason is obvious: Your grip is the only link between your body and the club, the club whose head impacts the ball. (Notice I didn't say "hits" the ball; I teach how to swing at the ball, not how to hit at the ball.)

THE GRIP

Grip the club with the left hand by coming at the shaft from the left side—not from above the shaft, not from below the shaft, but from the left side (see photos on pages 12 and 13). Grasp the shaft about an inch down from the top. Most golfers like to hold the club at its very end, but this prevents full control of the club when it is in motion.

Your left thumb will point straight down the shaft at the clubface. The thumb and forefinger grip the club very lightly. The last three fingers of the left hand, however, grip the club very, very firmly. Those are the guiding and supporting fingers.

Bring the right hand toward the clubshaft from the right side—not from below or above. The right hand will cover the

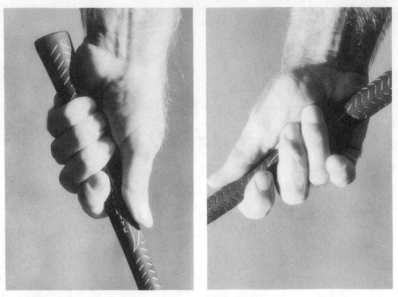

The left-hand grip.   **The right-hand grip.**

left thumb. The little pinky of the right hand, which isn't strong enough to go around the shaft, lies on top of the left hand. The right thumb points straight down the shaft. The thumb and forefinger grip the club very, very firmly. The other three fingers hold the club lightly.

You hold the club firmly, but it is not a choking grip. When you swing, your hands must have flexibility that will be reduced by a choking grip. Hold the club so that there is pressure only with the last three fingers of the left hand and the first finger and thumb of the right hand.

You are trying to get your two hands to act as one in swinging the club. Both thumbs should be pointing straight down the shaft so that the V's formed by the thumb and forefinger of each hand are pointing to a spot between your right ear and right shoulder.

Practice: Anywhere, any time. The grip is so important that you must grip a club as often as possible. Even then, do as the touring pros do: Check your grip at least once a week to make sure a fault hasn't crept into your grip.

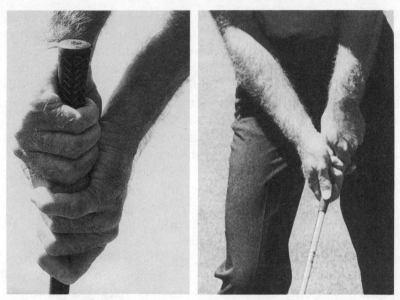

View from below of the overlapping grip.

View from above of the overlapping grip.

Lay the club so that it rests against your right leg. Grasp it first with the left hand, then with the right hand. Check your grip in a mirror and compare what you see with the photos on these pages. Practice gripping the shaft until you can grip the club without having to look down at your hands. Feel comfortable and also feel the pressure being exerted by the last three fingers of the left hand and the thumb and forefinger of the right hand. Check the V's formed by the thumb and forefingers. If you like, buy a practice grip so you can grip the shaft while watching TV or reading the newspaper. You want to impart to your muscle memory the feeling of a comfortable, yet firm, grip that makes two hands work like one hand.

THE STANCE

Later on, you will see how the stance may change for different clubs and different shots, but let's first get straight on the basic stance for all swings when the ball is not teed up. (The stance has to change for a teed-up ball since the tee shot is the only shot in golf in which the ball is already in the air.)

The ball sits smack in the middle of the stance, equidistant from both feet. The feet should be about shoulder width apart. Your weight is about evenly balanced: 50 percent on the front foot, 50 percent on the back foot.

Now place the clubhead behind the ball. I suggest you use a 5 iron or a 6 iron, as those clubs are about halfway between the longest-shafted clubs and the shortest-shafted clubs.

"How far should I stand from the ball?"

I hear that question most every time I give a lesson on the stance. We are all shaped differently, but the answer for all types—long, short, fat, and skinny—is a simple one: Stand so close to the ball that your feet are almost touching it. Now swing the club. You can't. Your midsection gets in the way of your arms, right? So shuffle both feet back two or three inches, or whatever it takes so that your arms swing freely and no longer brush your midsection. You are now standing the proper distance from the ball.

"How much should I bend over to reach the ball?"

That's another question I hear often. Again the answer is a simple one: You bend only slightly at the waist. But since a 9 iron is shorter than a driver, your hands are closer to the impact point when you address the ball with a 9 iron than they are when you hold a driver.

So we must bend to reach the ball with the clubhead of the shorter-shafted 9 iron. But we don't bend at the waist with the shorter clubs. We bend at the knees, assuming the position you would take if you were about to sit down on a stool.

Let me repeat this: With all clubs, we bend slightly at the waist to reach for the ball with the clubhead. *But the angle of the spine stays at the same angle, in relation to the ground, for all clubs—driver to wedge.* To get to the ball with the shorter clubs, we bend more at the knees—not more at the waist.

The most important things to remember about the stance are, first, that your nose and chin are on a line with the ball so that if the ball were directly below you, a coin dropped from the chin would land smack on the ball. And, secondly,

The square stance. Arms form a V, arms and shaft form a Y. Both feet touch a line that is parallel to the line to your target.

your two arms form a V (or, if you prefer, a Y with the club-shaft forming the bottom part of the Y).

Practice: Stand in front of a mirror with a 5 or 6 iron and a ball on the floor. Check to see that your feet are shoulder width apart, the weight evenly balanced, the nose and chin pointing directly at the ball—not behind it, not in front of it. The arms form a V or the arms and clubshaft form a Y. This is the square stance, and you will use it for most of your golf shots.

THE THREE-PHASE SWING

There are three phases—or three pieces, if you prefer—to the golf swing. There is the upswing. There is the downswing. There is the through swing.

As we progress, we will mesh these three pieces until they are one continuous golf swing.

I have said this before, I will say it here again, and I will say it later: You are not learning a golf hit, you are learning a golf swing. It is a golf swing, not a golf hit.

Go to a practice range (or anywhere you can hit a ball safely for a hundred yards or so) and tee up a ball.

Assume the proper grip and stance. Now you may say to yourself, "All right, little golf ball, now you are going to get it." And then you swing at the ball as hard as you can, let's say at a theoretical 60 miles an hour.

Chances are you already do that—most high handicappers do. You know the result: a topped shot, a shanked shot, a shot that brings color to the ears.

Or you may say to yourself, "I am going to swing at a nice, steady thirty miles an hour and I am going to count *one* and the club comes up; *two* and the club comes down; *three* and the club comes through." Chances are you will hit a shot that's airborne and straight toward a target.

If you want to hit a ball straight—and that's the first step toward breaking 100—then let's study what to do during the three phases of the swing:

Phase One

Most weekenders think of the first phase as the backswing. I want you to think of this phase as an *up* swing. Think this way: I am trying to get the club and my arms and hands up above the shoulders to build leverage and momentum. Think up. Don't think back.

Now, understand: I don't mean for you to pick up the club from the ball in a straight-up line. There must be some width and arc to the upswing. But this phase of the swing is basically upward so that the hands finish above the shoulders. Note that the hands do not finish behind or in back of the shoulders as they would for a baseball swing. They finish up above the shoulders. Again, think up, not back.

How high is up? The photo on this page shows my hands as high as they can go. But I have been doing this all my life, and I do a lot of stretching exercises. Your hands do not have to go that high. When your left shoulder touches your chin, that is the signal to you that your hands are high enough and that you have completed Phase One.

Phase One—the upswing— is completed when the left shoulder touches the chin.

Phase Two

Now we do the exact opposite of what we did in Phase One. Instead of thinking up, we now think down. This down action ends when we make contact with the ball. It should end *with your arms forming the V pattern (or the Y pattern with the arms and club) that was formed when you stood at address.* Your V-shaped arms placed the clubhead square to the ball at address. Those V-shaped arms must again place the clubhead square to the ball at impact—and thus start the ball off straight to your target.

Phase Two—the downswing—is completed at impact as the V-shaped arms re-form as they were formed at address, starting off the ball straight to its target.

Phase Three

This is the through part of the swing. Just after impact, the right shoulder passes under the chin—not in front of the chin as in a baseball swing. The arms continue to form the V (or the Y) until the hands and clubhead have come up to belt level. Then the clubhead, arms, and hands continue to rise, finishing above the left shoulder. Remember, as in the first phase, that this swing is an upward swing, not a backward swing. The hands and clubhead end up above the shoulders, not behind them.

Phase Three—the through swing—is an upward swing, the arms and hands forming the V until the clubhead is at belt level. This part of the through swing is completed when the right shoulder touches the chin.

TEMPO AND RHYTHM

In practicing the three phases, swing the club as fast as you can. You will shank, top, and otherwise mis-hit the ball. Now swing as slowly as you can. The ball will go only a few yards and you will have no sense of timing or rhythm.

Now swing the club about half as fast as when you swung the club very quickly. You are swinging now at a theoretical 30 miles an hour, not at a theoretical 60 miles an hour. You will get a sense of control—you can guide the clubhead to the ball—and you will feel the beginning of a sense of pace and rhythm.

Practice: Go to a driving range and swing through the three phases, concerned not with how far you hit the balls but with how straight you hit the balls. If the ball goes straight, the chances are that your swingpath is a correct one. Concentrating on the three phases, plus timing and rhythm, swat at least 60 balls.

At home, go to the backyard or any level ground. Place tees in the ground. Swing at the tees with an iron, keeping in mind the basics of the swing: up, down, through. If you flick the tees out of the ground so that they arc upward and outward a foot or so, you know you have made the proper swing.

DAY 2

The Lower Gear: The Feet, Knees, and Hips Coil or Pivot

Review the day 1 lesson briefly in your mind: Check your grip and the pressure points; review the stance with the ball in the middle of the feet and the weight evenly balanced; the three-phase swing that begins with the club going up above the shoulders, the club coming down so the arms re-form the V that they formed at address; and the right shoulder passing under the chin as the clubface comes up above the shoulders—not around the shoulders—in the through swing.

Today we introduce the turn (or pivot, or coil, or whatever description you like best). I call this the lower-gear action, with the ankles, feet, knees, hips, and shoulders coming into play to mesh with the upper-gear action.

How do we turn or pivot or coil?

The action begins with the left knee and left hip and left shoulder all angling in toward or *into* the ball—I repeat, *into* the ball—as the arms and hands and clubhead rise up above the shoulders on the upswing.

Very important: While the left knee, hip, and shoulder turn to point at the ball, there is a tendency to get loose and take the clubhead behind the shoulders. *Do not!* The clubhead must end up above the shoulders, not behind the shoulders. Otherwise, the clubhead starts off out of its proper swingpath.

This coiling action of the left side—the left knee, hip, and shoulder pointing directly behind the ball at the top of the upswing—has shifted the weight from about 50–50 to about

Lower-gear action begins with the left knee, hip, and shoulder angling toward—that is, into—the ball. The clubhead rises above the shoulders, not behind the shoulders.

60–40 or 70–30 in favor of the right leg. That leg will stand almost straight to hold the weight as the left knee is angling into the ball.

Another important point for weekenders: The left heel should stay as close to the ground as possible, even flat to the ground. If the left heel goes up more than a couple of inches, the club will likely go up a little high, and most weekenders then forget to lower the club during the downswing. So raise the left heel on the upswing no more than an inch, even less if possible. And by keeping the left heel down, the left ankle will help in turning the left side into the ball.

Now the downward motion begins. Your right shoulder, right hip, and right knee begin to point inward toward the ball. As your clubhead sweeps by the ball, your right knee is pointing at the ball and moving on quickly toward the target. So are your right foot, right hip, and right shoulder. And as your entire right side turns or coils to point toward the ball and then toward the target, most of your weight is shifting to the left leg. When you finish with hands high above the shoulders—not behind the shoulders—in the through swing, only the toe of your right foot is on the ground.

In the finish or follow-through of the swing, the forward movement of the club will bring your weight completely around from the right side to the left side. You finish the swing facing the target, not facing the ball.

But be cautious: Let the swing and the club bring you around. Don't try to use the body's weight shift or the pivot to bring the club around.

To repeat: The swing must bring you around from the right side to the left side so that the movement of the follow-through swing leaves you facing the target—not facing the original position of the ball.

If you look at the picture on page 27, you will see how you should finish the through swing. The hands are above the shoulders, and the belt buckle is turned so that it is facing the target and the line of flight. It is not—repeat *not*—facing the ball's original position.

This is the action of the lower gear.

Just before impact, the right knee is pointing at the ball and the entire right side is turning to point toward the ball and then toward the target.

Lower-gear action nears its finish as the right knee, hip, and shoulder turn toward the target, most of the weight shifting to the left leg. Only the toe of the right foot is on the ground.

Wrong! The through swing should not finish with the right shoulder passing, baseball-fashion, in front of the chin and with the hands finishing below the shoulders.

Now let me tell you how you can practice the action of the lower gear.

Practice: Stand in front of a mirror with a ball centered between your feet. Place your hands on your hips. Simulate the upswing by turning your left shoulder, your left hip, and left elbow. The left elbow should point to a position directly above the ball. Simulate the downswing by turning the right shoulder, right hip, and right elbow. The right elbow should point to a position directly above the ball.

Or try this exercise if you are supple enough: Place a club behind your back horizontally at waist level so that the shaft is gripped by both of your bent elbows. The clubhead points toward the target, and the club's grip points away from the target. Place both hands on your hips as you face the ball centered between your feet.

Turn, simulating the upswing. The clubhead should point to a spot above the ball. Now, turn and simulate the downswing. The club's grip should point to a spot above the ball. Practice this for 20-minute stretches as often as you can before your next session.

Correct! The through swing finishes with the right shoulder passing under the chin and the hands finishing high above the shoulders.

At impact, as at address, there must be a connecting rod—the straight left arm—connecting the left shoulder to the ball.

DAY 3

The Connecting Rod

Review the lower gear: The left knee points behind the ball on the upswing, and the right knee points ahead of the ball and toward the target on the downswing and the through swing.

Now we want to connect the lower gear to the upper gear. And the connecting rod between the lower gear and the upper gear is the straight and solid left arm coming down to meet the ball in the impact area.

If the left arm is bent or bowed at impact, the upper gear's power cannot connect with the lower gear's power. They will be moving independently of each other. If the upper gear has a theoretical power rating of two and the lower gear has a theoretical power rating of two, connecting the two together produces a theoretical power of four. But if they act independently of each other, you get two and two working against each other. And two minus two equals zero.

The two moves—upper gear and lower gear—must be brought together to make them into one fluid move. That connection is the straight left arm at impact. You must get the feeling that your left arm at impact is a straight and solid rod.

Practice: Do this without a club. Put the right hand behind the back. Simulate hitting the ball with the back of the left hand. Looking at a mirror, bring the left hand to the top of the upswing, that point where the left shoulder touches the chin. Don't worry if the left arm is crooked to some degree at the elbow.

Now bring the right shoulder, right hip, and right knee in toward the ball (centered in your stance) as you uncoil and bring down the "clubhead"—the back of your left hand. Stop the swing at the "impact" point. Check the mirror. Is the left arm straight? Continue to practice this move to get the feeling of bringing the clubhead down to the impact point, with the left arm as straight as the connecting rod it must be.

Second half of today's lesson: When you begin to get the feeling of a straight left arm at impact, let's go on to the next stage in making the connection between the upper gear and the lower gear.

Those two gears must stay connected after the clubhead impacts the ball and the through swing begins. They must stay connected to connect the ball to the target, whether that target be a spot on the fairway for a tee shot or a pin on the green for an approach shot.

So, please, don't bend or bow the left arm after impact, a fault of most 100-plus golfers. If the left arm bows after impact, the ball flies off to the right. The left arm must stay straight as the clubhead passes through the impact zone and rises to a point where the clubhead is as high as your belt buckle. With the left arm straight, this position is often called the "shaking-hands" position.

Let me repeat: 1) At impact, in order to get the ball airborne, you must have a connecting rod—that straight left arm—connecting the left shoulder to the ball. 2) After impact and during the first half of the through swing, there must also be a connecting rod—the straight left arm—connecting the airborne ball to the target, thus giving you accuracy.

Practice: As often as you can, whether in the living room or your backyard, use the back of the left hand as a clubface and check to see that the left arm stays straight from impact on into the shaking-hands position of the through swing. Then swing a club for another ten minutes, again checking to make sure that the left arm is straight from impact on into the shaking-hands position of the through swing.

Finally, here's a way to demonstrate to yourself the importance of what I call left-arm response.

Hold a club by its face so you can swing the butt end. Hold it with both hands. Swing the club using only your shoulders. What do you hear? Nothing, right?

The connecting rod—the straight left arm—connects the ball to the target during the first half of the through swing. The left arm stays straight until it reaches the "shaking-hands" position.

Wrong! Bending the left arm after impact will cause loss of distance and accuracy.

When only the shoulders swing the club, there is no whoosh. Swing with the left arm and you get full left-arm response.

Now grip the clubface with the left hand and take a simu-
lated upswing. Bring the clubhead down and you will hear the
whoosh sound that tells you that you are utilizing full left-arm
response.

When the body swings the club, there is no *whoosh,* meaning no left-arm response. Practice swinging the club with only
the left arm—not to build up muscles but to build up left-arm
response.

To sum up: The left arm can't pretzel at impact. It has to
stay straight at impact to mesh the power of the upper gear
and the lower gear and get the ball airborne. The left arm
must continue to stay straight—into the through swing to
provide a straight, accurate shot to the target. And, finally, the
left-arm response can't be sluggish or slow. Listen for that
*whoosh*ing sound that tells you that you are getting left-arm
response.

DAY 4

Think P-A-C-E, Think W-I-D-E

How fast do we swing on the upswing, how fast do we swing on the downswing, and how far do we swing on the through swing? That's what we want to get straight during this lesson.

We touched on pacing in our first lesson, but now I want to incorporate timing and rhythm—pacing, in short—into the two fundamentals we have learned: the action of the upper gear and the action of the lower gear.

Most people who have played golf for any length of time, or who have taken lessons, have had this thought drilled into them: Take the clubhead back *slowwwwwwwwwly*. An easy, gentle takeaway, an easy and slow upswing. That is good.

But what happens next? There is an understandable urge to be more aggressive on the downswing, a temptation to swing harder at that little white rascal. There is also the tendency to try to make up for the slowness of the upswing with extra speed on the downswing. If the golfer takes up the club at 20 miles an hour, he is tempted to take down the club at 60 miles an hour. The result is an uncontrollable swing, a mis-hit, the ball slicing off to the golfer's right or hooking off to his or her left.

But if you have played golf for a while, you also know what you usually do when you take a practice swing on a fairway. You face, let's say, a 5 iron shot of about 160 yards to the green. You stand away from the ball, take a nice and slow upswing and an equally paced downswing. If you took the clubhead back at 20 miles an hour, you probably bring the club down at no more than 35 or 40 miles an hour. You take the club down reasonably close to the same speed you took the club up.

Why is that? Because there was no ball to smash on the practice swing, no little rascal to crush. But when you step up to the ball for the actual swing, there—again—is that awful temptation on the downswing to swing 60 miles an hour.

The pace of the upswing and the pace of the downswing should be thought of in the same terms as a swinging pendulum of a grandfather's clock. The pendulum swings right at the same pace . . . *tick*. It swings left at the same pace . . . *tock*. Tick, tock, tick, tock.

Now, it is only natural to be more aggressive—and thus swing harder—on the downswing. But if you can think of that equal tick-tock rhythm or pace for the upswing and the downswing, you will not swing at three times the pace of the upswing. If you swing at two times the pace of the upswing, you are getting closer to the controllable downswing that will produce the same clubface contact with the ball that you had at address.

In short, we want to make the pace of the downswing as close as possible to the pace of the upswing. Then you will have a swing that is controllable, for one thing, and—most important—you will be getting closer to owning a swing that you can repeat and repeat and repeat during any one round of golf.

And the swing that you can repeat time after time is a key to breaking 100. After all, even the 120 golfer will hit two or three good golf shots during a round. But that's not really playing golf. We want to hit those good shots time and time again so that we can go a round under 100 shots.

I call "tempo" or "pacing" the intangible of a golf swing— an intangible that is not easy for all golfers to master right away. I tell my students that if you feel you are taking the club up extra slow, add a little momentum to the upswing. Try to make up for that extra momentum by taking about the same amount of momentum away from the downswing. Then you are on your way to equalizing as much as possible the downswing with the upswing. Get the upswing and the downswing closer to the balance of that tick-tock-tick-tock rhythm of a pendulum.

Practice: At home, in the backyard, or at a practice range, take nothing but practice swings. Swing the club with no ball on the ground, no ball to crush. Watch your shadow if it is a sunny day, or watch yourself in a mirror at home, or have someone observe you. Practice 15 to 20 minutes at keeping the downswing no more than twice the pace of the upswing. Once you feel you are close to this pendulumlike rhythm, then put down a ball and try to swing at the same pace—no more than twice the speed of the upswing for the downswing.

Once you have your upswing and downswing in tempo, turn to the through swing.

If one word describes the upswing, it is *up.*

If one word describes the downswing, it is *descending.*

If one word describes the through swing, it is *wide.*

Wide. Look at the photo of my swing (page 38) as I go through to the hand-shake position. The distance from my left side to my left hand is as wide as it could possibly be. It is not cramped or close. This W-I-D-E through swing gives you two things: it gives the ball distance because you have not quit on the shot and lost or diminished the speed of the clubhead. And you have gained accuracy because the straight left arm is now the connection between the target and the airborne ball.

One last word on the pacing of the downswing and the pacing of the through swing. It is a down-and-through swing. Tempo must make these two phases of the swing into one phase.

Furthermore, the through swing and the downswing must be given equal force. Let me explain: If you use 70 percent of your force on the downswing, you will get the ball up, but there is only 30 percent of your force left to give the ball distance. The ball won't go very far, and it may go left or right instead of straight.

If you use 30 percent of your force on the downswing, the ball will not go very high. And if you use the remaining 70

One word describes the through swing: W-I-D-E. A wide through swing gives distance and accuracy.

percent of your force on the through end of the swing, you will only be adding force to a shot that will travel most of its distance through the grass, which will slow it down.

Try to get 50 percent of your force into the downswing and 50 percent of your force into the through portion of the swing. And think of imparting 100 percent of your force to a down-and-through swing.

Practice: To get the feeling of making the through swing wide, place two tees on the ground about six inches apart. Put a target ball on the tee that's placed in the middle of your stance, and a second ball on the tee that's opposite your front toe.

Swing at the target ball. As you impact it, continue through so that you impact the second ball. If you reach the second ball, then your through swing is as wide as it should be.

You can practice adding that width to your through swing in the backyard by placing two tees in the ground, one in the middle of your stance, the other off your front toe. If you swat both tees out of the ground, you are getting the proper width to your through swing. You are not quitting at impact.

DAY 5

Light Fire to the Clubhead

If you have practiced the fundamentals of what we worked on in the first four days, you are now hitting nice-looking shots. But the ball is not going very far. And golf courses are made up of 550-yard holes, along with the 125-yarders. No golf course is a pitch-and-putt affair.

So now, assuming you have mastered the fundamentals to some degree, let's put spark and fire to your club and a "click" or zing to your shots.

But before I begin, let me restate my now-familiar reminder: We are learning a golf swing, not a golf hit. We do not send a ball longer by hitting it harder. What gives a clubhead spark and fire is the utilization of the hands and wrists.

What does that mean?

Let's go back to the upswing. If we turn properly so that the hands, clubhead, and arms rise above the shoulders, the arms and wrists bend naturally at the top of the upswing. The wrists set naturally; they take care of themselves.

The change—that is, the straightening of the wrists to the position they had been in at address—takes place on the way down. True enough, the wrists would straighten on their own to some extent on the way down as the clubhead comes into the ball. In fact, if the grip on the top of your clubshaft is in line with the clubhead at impact, meaning the wrists are now just as straight as they were at address, you will get a nice, straight shot—but one without any great distance, no fire leaping from its tail.

Now, understand: Up to now you should be contacting the ball just as you contacted it at address. If the grip of your clubshaft is in line with the clubhead at impact, we get a nice, straight shot.

But now we are ready to go beyond that—to what the pros call the "late hit," the "secret" to long drives.

The answer: You give spark to your shots by utilizing the hands and wrists. That means straightening the wrists not at impact, but somewhere during the downswing.

Here's why: Put the clubface against the ball as you would at address. The club's grip (at the top of the shaft) is in line with the clubhead. The result, as I said, is a straight shot.

Now move the clubhead a few inches to the right. Straighten out your wrists. After you straighten your wrists, contact the ball. As contact is made, the clubhead has moved in front of the grip.

That straightening of the wrists before impact—and not at impact—results in a "snapping" of the wrists. And that straightening or snapping motion gives spark and zing to your shot, adding an extra 10 to 30 or more yards of distance.

To repeat: *If the grip is in line with the clubhead at impact, you get a straight but sparkless, droopy shot. But if the clubhead moves ahead of the grip just before impact, snapping the clubhead into the ball, you get a shot with zing to it.*

OK so far?

But you have an obvious question: At what point in the downswing do you straighten your wrists?

For the answer, let's go back again—this time to the address position. Standing there, you know that your shoulders are about level with each other. After the clubhead comes upward in the upswing, the right shoulder rises higher than the left. As you start the downswing, the right shoulder begins to come down. Somewhere in the downswing, the right shoulder and the left shoulder are level again—as level as they were at address.

Ostroske holds a club with his left hand to show how the right shoulder drops below the level of the left shoulder during the downswing. At this point, the right shoulder has just dropped below the left and the grip is still ahead of the clubhead.

When the right shoulder drops below the left on the downswing, the clubhead moves ahead of the grip and the wrists straighten for the "late release." That produces the "snapping" action that lights fire to the clubhead and adds distance to the shot.

Now, listen up. At the point when your right shoulder drops *below* the left shoulder during the downswing, the club has entered the impact area.

It's then that you release the wrists. You straighten them. This will put the clubhead in front of the grip.

Obviously, you can't see that right shoulder drop below the left during the downswing. You have other things to look at, notably the ball. You must *feel* that right shoulder drop below the left shoulder.

Then you release your wrists—that is, you straighten the wrists. You get the late hit, you put fire into your clubhead— and zing goes your shot.

Knowing when to release the wrists can only come with practice. Before the next lesson, spend at least an hour working on sensing when the right shoulder has dropped below the left in the downswing.

Practice: Stand in front of a mirror and watch your downswing. As you make the downswing in slow motion, see when the right shoulder drops below the left. Then, still in slow motion, straighten the wrists so that the clubhead moves in front of the grip.

Go outside and swing on a sunny day. Watch your shadow. See when the right shoulder drops below the left. Or ask someone, as they watch you swing slowly at first but gradually a little faster, to tell you the moment when the right shoulder dips below the left.

Knowing when to straighten or release the wrists—at the moment the right shoulder drops—can only come to you by feel. But once you hit a shot with the clubhead in front of the grip, you will know you have straightened the wrists at the right instant. And, along with a wide and complete through swing—finishing with the club above your shoulders—you will feel a major difference in your shots. You will feel that zing, that click, that fire now adding distance to your game in shot after shot.

DAY 6

The Swing's Sweet 16 Fundamentals

This is the last day in the "classroom." Over the past five days, we have gone over the fundamentals of the golf swing. Starting tomorrow, we will go to the course and begin work on the specific shots, including—during days 7, 8, and 9—a look at the three quickest ways to shave strokes off your score.

Today, then, let's go over the highlights of what we have learned. When we step onto the course tomorrow, I don't expect you to remember (without peeking at the book) all the things I have told you during the past five days. But know these 16 fundamentals cold. If you can, Xerox these 16 reminders; stuff the paper in your pocket so you can look them over if you feel your swing is coming apart at any time during the next two weeks of lessons.

1. Check your grip. The V's formed by thumbs and forefingers point to the right shoulder. Pressure is firm with the last three fingers of the left hand and the forefinger and thumb of the right hand. Both hands feel like they are working as one.
2. The face of your club sits square to your target. The toe of the club is not—repeat, *not*—pointing in toward your feet or out away from your feet.
3. Both feet are planted in a square stance so the toes touch an imaginary line that is parallel to the line connecting the ball to your target.

4. The ball is positioned between both feet (when the ball is not teed up) and the feet are shoulder width apart.

5. Both arms are straight, forming a V pattern.

6. Bend slightly at the waist for all clubs. Get closer to the ball with shorter clubs by bending at the knees, adopting a sitting position. Don't bend at the waist to get closer to the ball.

7. Phase One of the swing is back and up, not up and back. The upswing ends when your left shoulder touches the chin. At that point, the club and hands and arms must be above the shoulders.

8. Phase Two is coming down with the club so that both arms return to re-form that V shape as the clubhead impacts the ball.

9. Phase Three is through and up, the club and hands and arms finishing above the shoulders, not behind or around the shoulders, as in a baseball swing. When the right shoulder touches the chin, that is the signal the through swing has ended.

10. The movement of the upper gear—club, hands, arms, and shoulders—is up, down, then up and through.

11. The lower gear—feet, knees, and hips—comes into play to provide turn and weight shift. As the club comes up from the ball, the movement is a turning upswing. You turn the left knee and left hip in toward the ball. This pitches your weight back to the right leg and gives you a windup position with the arms and shoulders.

12. As you come down with the club, the right hip and right knee turn into the ball—*in* is again the key word. This turning downswing pitches your weight toward the left side.

13. As you impact the ball and the club begins to come up and through, the right hip and right knee continue to turn and only stop turning when they face the target. Your weight has now shifted completely to the left side, the toe of your right foot the only part of your right side on the ground. Key point to remember: After impact, the right hip and right knee continue to turn to face the target. They do not stop so that the right knee, after impact, is pointing to the ball's original position.

14. Tempo means taking a swing that is not so fast that all the pieces of the action don't have time to fit together in proper sequence. Nor is the tempo so slow that there is no feeling of rhythm to the swing. Being too slow is as bad as being too fast. A proper tempo is one in which the speed of the upswing matches as closely as possible the speed of the downswing. (It is only natural for the downswing to be faster, because you want to get the ball up and going. But it should not be three times faster, not even two times faster.) Practice swinging down at the same speed you swing up, and you will get close to matching the speed of the downswing with the speed of the upswing.

15. Are you meshing the action of the upper gear with the action of the lower gear? If they don't mesh, you lose distance and you lose accuracy. The rod that connects both gears is the straight left arm at impact. Check constantly that the left arm is straight at impact.

16. Now we are hitting straight shots for reasonable distance. To get more distance—and break 100—we need to add zing to the shot with the so-called "late hit." When, on the downswing, your right shoulder dips below the left shoulder, your clubhead has entered the impact area. At that point, you straighten out or release your wrists to get the clubhead ahead of the grip at impact. That produces the "snapping" action of the clubhead that adds ten to 30 yards to a shot. But this "late hit"—the release or straightening of the wrists—must be enhanced by a high and full and W-I-D-E follow-through that ends with the arms, hands, and clubhead above the shoulders—not, as in a baseball swing, behind the shoulders.

Master these 16 key fundamentals so they come more or less naturally to you. Now, let's grab a 6 iron and charge for that 100 barrier.

DAY 7

The Pitch-and-Run: Your Best Way to Shave Strokes from a 100-Plus Score

You could face this shot on every hole. By making it, you can leave yourself time after time with one-putt greens.

The pitch-and-run can make you the equal of a low handicapper who shoots in the 80s. On a par-4 hole, he hits his second shot to the green. If you're like most high handicappers, your third shot lands short of the green—in the fringe about ten to 20 yards off the green, maybe 20 to 30 yards from the pin.

The low handicapper two-putts for his par 4. You pitch your shot onto the green and the ball runs to within two feet of the cup. You sink that putt for your 5—which is your equivalent of his par 4. If you can shoot one over par on every hole, remember, you will come in with a nine-oh. Yes, a 90.

Mastering the pitch-and-run can give you a par to match the low handicapper's par on a par-3 hole. Let's say, on a 150-yard hole, he or she hits to the green, then two-putts for par. You hit onto the grass behind the green. You pitch-and-run the ball to within two feet of the cup, then sink the putt and you, too, have a par 3.

Most high handicappers hit their approach shots short of the green. That's not always too damaging to a score. What sends a score soaring is this: You hit your next shot so short that the ball lands on the edge of the green and now you need at least two putts to hole out. It cost you three strokes to go about 30 to 40 yards. Or you hit the shot too hard and the ball stops on the grass on the other side of the green. Now you stand in the same position you were in before you hit the shot—and you have wasted one stroke. You may take three more strokes to hole out—a total of four when you should have holed out in two.

That's why I can't think of a better way to shave off strokes than mastering the pitch-and-run. The pros call it "down in two."

The first key to executing this shot: Take it easy, take it slow. You've come a long way, perhaps 300 to 500 yards. Now take it easy. Judge how far you stand from the pin. If there's time, pace off the yardage—one stride being one yard. Let's say you stride off 20 yards. Now stride back ten yards along the target line. That is the spot on the green where you want the ball to land. You want to pitch the ball halfway to the target through the air—there are no bumps, no slopes, no pebbles in the air—and then roll the ball the rest of the way on the smooth green carpet to the pin.

I suggest you choose a 7 iron. It has the right degree of loft and, with a proper follow-through, it will give you the right amount of run. Remind yourself: We will not be making a full swing; like a putt, this will strictly be a hands-and-arms swing, no body motion whatever.

1. Ball is in the center of the stance.
2. The feet are close together.
3. The stance is square (meaning the feet are lined up on a line that is parallel to the target line).
4. On the upswing, bring the clubhead back about knee high and about two feet beyond your right foot.
5. On the downswing, contact the ball as the blade sweeps under the ball. You don't slice into the turf; that is, you don't take a divot.

Mechanics of the pitch-and-run: Bring the clubhead back about knee high, contact the ball as the blade sweeps under the ball, follow through (opposite page) so the clubhead comes up about knee high. The swing is strictly hands and arms.

6. And now—most important—follow through so that the clubhead ends about two feet beyond the left toe. As in all golf shots, you match the upswing with the through swing.

If, as you practice this shot, you consistently pitch the ball beyond your landing area, choke down more on the club, even to where you are grasping the metal part of the shaft. Remind yourself that you are swinging with the same motion

with which you putt, the exceptions being that the clubhead comes higher on the upswing and the through swing and you are hitting with a lofted club.

Remember this above all: Execute this shot slowly. Take your time about planning where you want the pitch to land on the green. Bring back the club slowly. Come through the ball slowly. Finish the through swing slowly.

Practicing the pitch-and-run. Place two parallel clubs halfway to the hole and practice landing the ball between the clubs.

Practice: Stand from ten to 20 yards off a putting green and place two clubs about halfway between you and the pin. Place the clubs so they run on a parallel line to your target line (the line from the ball to the pin). Land at least five out of ten balls onto a spot between the two clubs.

When you are reasonably satisfied with your pitching accuracy, concentrate on practicing the "run" half of the shot. Hit ten balls that land halfway. Make sure that you follow through so that at least five of the ten balls roll to within two feet of the pin.

Anyone, weak or strong, weekender or pro, can execute the pitch-and-run—your best way to save strokes that will get your score below 100.

DAY 8

Putting: Your Next Best Way to Shave Strokes

We know that 40 percent of the average golfer's strokes are taken on the putting green. That's one strong argument for giving a lot more time, perhaps close to 40 percent, to practicing the sinking of short and medium putts while also practicing the lagging of longer putts close enough to drop in two.

Here's a second argument: Anyone can putt. Be you frail or muscled, fat or skinny, coordinated or tangle-footed, you can putt a ball into a hole as accurately as a Palmer, a Nicklaus, or a Strange. The putter, like the cowboy's six-gun, is The Great Equalizer.

A stroke is a stroke, whether it's one that carries a ball 270 yards off a tee, or one that rolls a ball one inch into a cup. If your partner hits a ball 200 yards to a green for one stroke, while you need two strokes to go those 200 yards, he's one stroke up on you. But if he takes two strokes to roll the ball ten feet into the hole and you need only one stroke to go those ten feet, you and he are now even. The Great Equalizer.

And those one-putt greens and two-putt greens will work magic in dropping your score below the 100 level. If you average three putts a hole, that's 54 strokes, making it impossible for you to break 100. But if you average three putts a hole for nine holes and two putts a hole for the other nine, that's 45 strokes in the round. You have 54 strokes left to break 100. That's an average of three strokes a hole from tee to green, which is do-able.

The more two-putt (and one-putt) greens, obviously, the more likely you can smash the 100 barrier. So let's get down to the basics of putting:

1. Feet close together, as close as an inch or two for short putts, up to about eight to ten inches for longer putts.
2. Eyes over the ball so that a plumb line from the nose would drop onto the ball.
3. At address, the putterface is square to the target line— the line from ball to target. The putterface may turn slightly as the club is drawn back, but it must return to be at a right angle to the target line at impact. And it must stay at a right angle to the target line well into the through swing.
4. The putting swing is like all golf swings. In fact, it is a golf swing in miniature. The club comes straight back (instead of up). It comes straight ahead (instead of down). And it comes straight through (instead of through and up).
5. There is no body movement. Only the hands and arms— not the wrists or shoulders—are moving. Hands and arms move in a pendulumlike motion—again, a miniature version of the full golf swing.
6. While your head must not move until well after impact, it is especially important that the knees and shoulders also do not move at any point until well into the follow-through. If the shoulders or the kneecaps move, the head is also likely to move and draw the putterhead off the target line.
7. The putterhead must stay close to the ground during the three phases, rising only slightly off the grass at the end of the straight-back phase and at the end of the through-swing phase.
8. On all putts, no matter the length, the ends must match up. Thus, if you draw the clubhead three inches past the right toe on the straight-back phase, bring the clubhead three inches past the left toe at the end of the follow-through phase.

Avoid wristiness except in the longest putts. The most consistent putters are the putters who use the pendulum

Pendulum putting. At address, the feet are close together, eyes directly over the ball.

Take the putterface back still square (at a 90-degree angle) to the target line.

Keep the putterface square during and after impact and make the follow-through match the distance of the takeaway. If you take the putter back two inches beyond the right toe on the takeaway, bring the clubhead two inches beyond the left toe on the follow-through.

motion: Their hands and arms move past the body going back and move past the body going through. Jabbing—that is, quitting on the putt midway through the follow-through—will inevitably knock the putt off line. So will moving the putterhead at impact so the toe points away from you: The putt will roll to the right of the line. If the putterhead's toe points toward you, the ball will roll to the left of the line.

On day 15, we will discuss reading the green and putting strategy for long, intermediate, and short putts. But before we leave the practice green today, let me say this about putts of varying lengths: On all putts your stance is square. That is, your feet, knees, hips, and shoulders are set square to a line that is parallel to the line from the ball to your target. On longer putts, you may hold the club nearer the end, while on short putts it is a good idea to come down on the grip for more control. On short putts, I exert a little more pressure on the shaft with the thumbs, again for more control. On all putts, we strike the ball—not at the bottom as we do for most shots—but midway up the ball, at what's called the "equator" of the ball. Unlike most golf shots, we don't want backspin on our putts. We want overspin so the ball will roll. So we hit the flattest part of the ball. Some pros say they imagine there's a tack stuck in the back of the ball at the equator and they are using their putter to smack the tack into the ball.

Luck has to help when you sink putts longer than ten feet. But what we must do on these long putts is coax the ball close enough to the cup to sink it with your second putt. Most pros aim for a circle no more than two feet in radius around the hole.

On intermediate putts—those of four to ten feet—you definitely want to make a high percentage. I watch the cup before I putt, because I want to make sure that the ball gets at least to the cup. If it doesn't reach the cup, the ball can't go in. Never up, as we say, never in.

On short putts—those under four feet—I definitely want to make a high percentage—at least 70 percent. You should figure, in trying to break 100, on making more of these short

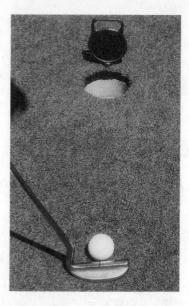

On short putts, strike the ball so firmly that it will hit an imaginary "backboard" and rebound into the hole.

putts than you miss. I grip the club firmly and I aim for the back of the cup. I think of the cup as having a basketball backboard at its rear. I want to hit the ball so firmly that the ball will hit the backboard and "rebound" into the cup. In short, I want the putt to have enough steam so that it won't come up short. Never up, never in.

Another reason why I want the putt to have enough steam: I don't want the putt to weaken near the hole. An imperfection around the hole—a spike mark, a tuft of grass—could cause the ball to veer away from the cup or stop short of the hole.

Practice: Line up five balls on a putting green. Place the first ball six inches from the cup, the second 12 inches, the third 18 inches, the fourth 24 inches, and the fifth 30 inches. Attempt to sink the balls in succession. If you miss a putt, replace all five balls in their original positions and begin again. Putt all five balls into the hole at least three times.

Place the balls in a circle about eight feet from the hole. Knock in at least two of the eight. Do this three times in a row.

Place five balls in a circle about 20 feet from the hole. Putt all five balls so that at least three of the five come to a stop within two feet of the cup. Do this at least three times.

DAY 9

Blasting Out of Sand: It's One-Two Easy

Every 100-plus golfer knows the frustration of hitting a ball out of one sand trap, straight across a green—and into another sand trap. What should have cost you one stroke now will cost you a second, a third, maybe even a fourth stroke. When I say that learning to blast out of sand traps onto a green for a one-putt or a two-putt green can save you at least three to five strokes a round, I am probably guilty of an understatement. For many weekenders, blasting from greenside traps to greens in one stroke can be the biggest stroke saver of all.

Watch the pros on TV and you will notice that when they enter a bunker, they shuffle their feet and dig in the soles of their shoes. They want a good, solid foundation. You don't want to be standing on the top of the sand and slide when you swing. Dig down until you can feel good, firm footing in the sand.

The sand shot is a unique one in golf. It is the only shot in which you hit the ground first and then the ball. Secondly, like the tee shot, it is the only swing in golf in which you contact the ball not with a descending blow, but as the club is rising. You catch the ball on the upswing and the follow-through.

What this means: You must position the ball, when blasting out of sand, so that it is lined up opposite the left toe. This allows you to catch the ball on the upswing.

At address for the bunker blast, the ball is positioned off the left toe, feet are close together and shuffled deep into the sand, and the clubface is open.

Also, keep in mind that we are not shooting for distance; we are trying to loft the ball onto anywhere on the green.

The sand wedge is the club you must use for all blasts out of greenside bunkers. The sand wedge has a very wide bottom (flange), and by positioning the ball up front, you utilize the weight and size of the flange. You want the flange to bounce off the sand rather than dig into the sand and stop the follow-through. Stopping the follow-through is the biggest sin you can make when you blast out of sand. It is an error that will almost inevitably leave you with the need for another stroke—or two or three—to get you onto something green.

The clubface of the sand wedge should be open. By open I mean turning the face so that the face is as parallel to the ground as the face permits. You are getting, as a result, as much loft out of the club as possible—and what you want, for this lob shot, is loft. Not distance—loft.

Now let's go through the keys for the successful blast out of sand.

1. Feet close together and shuffled deep in the sand.
2. Face of the sand wedge is open—that is, parallel to the ground.
3. On the upswing and the downswing and the through swing, there is no body motion at all. You do not make a pivot or a turn on the backswing, you do not make a pivot or a turn on the downswing, you do not make a pivot or a turn on the through swing. *This is strictly a movement of the arms and wrists.*
4. You are not in any hurry at all. The tempo is three quarters of the pace of the normal swing. There is a tendency to think you must swing very hard to blast the ball out of the sand. The reverse is true. Swing slowly but with precision, hitting the sand behind the ball. Let the weight of the flange do the muscle work, not the force of your swing.
5. As we start the upswing, the wrists break early. The hands must rise above the belt but not rise above the shoulders. The clubhead, however, will reach a point above the shoulders and point toward the target.
6. On the downswing, the wrists straighten—or uncock—

The swing is strictly a movement of the arms and wrists with no body motion at all. Impact the sand first, then the ball.

early, at the point the clubhead has passed the level of your belt.

7. You contact the sand first, an inch to two inches behind the ball. Remember that the more sand you contact, the shorter the ball will travel to the green.

8. The follow-through is the most important key to this shot. The follow-through, as in all golf shots, matches the distance of the upswing. But when you blast out of a deep trap, the follow-through should exceed the distance of the upswing so that your hands and the clubhead rise, if possible, *above the lip of the bunker.* The higher the lip of the bunker, in other words, the higher the through swing. Too many weekenders quit on this shot, thinking that contact with the sand and the ball does the job. Remember that you are shoveling a spray of sand, along with the ball, to the green. As with any shoveling motion, you must complete the shoveling motion with a follow-through.

Many pros will tell you that the sand blast is one of the easiest shots in golf. They say, "After all, this is the only shot in golf where you don't have to hit the ball."

That's true, but I can understand why the sand blast is a scary one for most weekenders. You are on foreign soil, standing on sand instead of grass. You are asked to do the opposite of what you have been taught to do: hit the ground first, then the ball. (And the rules say you can't even touch the sand until you swing!)

A few years ago, I was having trouble blasting accurately out of sand. A friend, a touring pro, gave me a tip that helped me greatly. He told me to practice blasting out of sand while standing on only one foot. Almost immediately, I began to blast to the pin. Here's why: I had to swing slowly or I would fall on my face. And since my one-footed stance was so weak, I had to follow through so I could get the ball out of the trap.

Swing slowly. Follow through. No longer will you blast so strong that you land the ball in another trap. Nor will you blast so weakly that you end up in the same trap. Let's not leave strokes in the sand of greenside bunkers. Remember: Swing slowly. Follow through.

Follow through so the hands and clubhead rise, if possible, above the lip of the bunker.

Practice: Find a sandy area, a beach, a child's sandbox (when the children are somewhere else) or a range that has a practice bunker. Place a target no more than 15 or 20 yards away. Blast balls to that target, keeping the two keys in mind: 1) a slow-motion swing that will leave the ball short of the target at first, but gradually—as you pick up speed—closer to the target; 2) a full through swing that leaves your hands above the lip of the bunker or, if the lip is too high, above your eye level.

DAY *10*

Hitting Off the Tee: A Game of Contradictions

First, the answers to two commonly asked questions:

Question number one: Should I hit off the tee with a driver or a 3 or 4 wood?

The 1 wood has the longest shaft of all the clubs in your bag. Make a mistake with it—say, a slight bend in the left arm's "connecting rod" at impact—and that mistake is magnified at the impact point and at the landing area. A mistake that throws you off 20 yards with another club could throw you off 40 yards with the driver.

But, yes, you must learn to hit off the tee with the driver if you are going to break 100. The driver is the club designed to give you the distance off the tee, and that's what you need to break 100. My advice is this: Start a round swinging the 3 or 4 wood off the tee. After a few holes, as you warm up and get more confidence in your swing, switch to the driver.

Question number two: How high do I tee up the ball? That is dictated by the club you use. Some drivers are thin-headed, others own jumbo-size heads. Tee up the ball so that half of the ball is above the head. In short, not too high, not too low.

We make one fundamental change in our stance when we address the ball on a tee. We line up the ball so that it is positioned off our left heel, not in the center of the stance where it would be for a fairway shot. Why? Because the ball on the tee is already in the air. This is a game of contradictions: When we want the ball to go up, we hit down. The sharper the angle we hit down, the steeper the angle the ball

Line up the ball for the tee shot so it is positioned off the left heel. Think S-L-O-W upswing and downswing.

goes up. So when a ball is on the ground, we address it in the middle of our stance so we can impact the ball with a descending blow.

But now, on the tee, the ball is in the air. We want to impact the ball as the clubhead comes through the impact area at the bottom of the swing's arc or even as the clubhead begins to rise. For this to happen, we position the ball opposite our left heel—in short, more up front where the clubhead will catch the ball at the bottom of the swing or at the start of the upswing and drive the ball off the tee.

Standing at the tee, facing a green perhaps 500 yards away, it is a natural inclination to think, "I have to swing as hard and fast as I can on this shot. I have got to gobble up a lot of yardage."

Again: This is a game of contradictions. The more distance you want from a club, the more slowly you swing the club. Why? Because the driver is designed and built to be a distance club. It has distance built into its long shaft and massive clubhead. We swing the club slowly so we can give the club the time to use all of its features—its shaft, its heavy clubhead—to do the work in giving us distance. Your tools are not your muscles, your tools are the club.

The takeaway and upswing swing, then, are a touch slower than usual, but it is the same back- and upswing. We reach the top of the upswing when the left shoulder touches the chin, making sure that the hands, arms, and club are above the shoulders.

The downswing matches the upswing in tempo and speed as closely as possible—*not*, certainly, more than twice as fast on the downswing compared to the upswing. This is especially important when swinging the driver, because we 1) want to sweep the ball rather than impact it with a descending blow as we do when the ball is on the ground; and 2) it is vital at impact to have our "connecting rod"—that left arm—perfectly straight.

At impact, when hitting off the tee, the weekender tends to quit on the shot. He hears the "click" of clubhead against ball and thinks the job is done.

That's a mistake for any shot, but it is an especially fatal mistake when swinging the driver. On shots from the fairway,

Concentrate on being W-I-D-E for the through swing and give 60 percent instead of the usual 50 percent into driving the ball after impact.

when the ball is on the ground, we have two equal jobs—to get the ball up into the air and then "send" it a certain distance to the target. So we give about 50 percent of our force to the descending blow that gets the ball up and about 50 percent of our force to the through swing that gives the ball distance and accuracy.

But the tee shot is unique in golf: The ball is already in the air before we impact it. Therefore, we should give perhaps only 40 percent of our force to the downswing, the tee having given us the other 10 percent. We give 60 percent of our force to driving the ball. After all, isn't that why we are at the tee—to *drive* the ball?

So, instead of quitting on the tee shot, concentrate on being W-I-D-E on the through swing. Do not leave your energy at the ball; send your energy, send the club as you swing W-I-D-E to the target.

Now, remember again: This is a golf swing, not a golf hit, even though your drives are your longest shots. Let the club, and a full, wide swing, *send* the ball.

Banish from your mind, as you go to a tee box, that you must throw a Sunday punch at that little white fellow on the tee.

Instead, think S-L-O-W upswing. Think downswing matching the upswing in tempo as much as possible. Think straight left arm at impact to connect the upper and lower gears. And most important, think wide through swing that sends the ball while also connecting the ball to its target. Result: a long, straight drive. And a long, straight drive, on any hole, is your first giant step toward breaking 100.

Practice: Using the driver, place two tees in the ground in your backyard or anywhere. Place the tees about six inches apart. Taking a slower-paced swing than usual, even a slow-motion-type upswing and downswing, clip the first tee and continue the swing to clip the second tee. Increase the speed of the upswing and downswing gradually, concentrating on clipping both tees. You will be imparting into your muscle memory the importance of a slow upswing and downswing and a wide through swing—the three basics of long and accurate drives.

DAY 11

Fairway Woods: Remember Who's Boss—It's the Upper Gear!

Weekenders ask me what woods they should carry in their bag in addition to the driver. I suggest a 3 or 4 wood, depending on whichever loft you prefer, plus a utility wood like a 6 or a 7 for getting out of the rough. The club can be wood or one of the new metal models. A 3 or 4 wood will give you distance on the fairway when the ball is sitting reasonably high in the grass. When it's set down lower, or sits in short rough, you will probably be safer swinging with the more lofted, smaller-headed 6 wood or 7 wood.

Avoid what I see too many weekenders doing when they set up for a fairway-wood shot. One, they take a wider stance, figuring that's the "power stance" they need for a shot of 150 to 200 yards. Secondly, especially with the longer-shafted woods, they take the club back and up instead of up and back on the upswing. Result: The club ends up behind their shoulders instead of above the shoulders. What follows is a round-house swing that strikes the ball a glancing blow—and a slice to the right or a hook to the left.

The stance should be no more than shoulder width, as it is for most any other shot. A wider stance does not allow the body to work as it should, and what you get is less power instead of more power.

Most weekenders fear they will not get the ball airborne with a wood off the fairway. The fear is understandable: A 3 wood is not as lofted as a 5 or 6 iron. And yet you must swing the fairway wood as you would swing a fairway iron, hitting the ball with a descending blow that gets the ball up.

What too many weekenders do, therefore, is use the lower gear—the legs and the torso—to bend at the knees and swing with the right side of the body. In effect, they try to scoop the ball to get it airborne. The result is inevitably a botched shot that goes left or right, short, or no place.

In the golf swing, the upper gear must be dominant. This is especially true when swinging the longer-shafted clubs like the fairway woods. The arms and hands and shoulders must do more of the work than the lower body, the hips and knees. It is the upper gear that puts the *whiz* into the swing, the *whiz* that sends a ball.

The key to swinging the fairway woods, then, is meshing the downswing with the through swing. The best tip that I can give you in swinging fairway woods: Apply 50 percent of your force to the downswing and make sure you have 50 percent left over for the go-through swing. The swing is up, down, and through, in that order, but getting the ball up with a fairway wood means applying half your force to bringing down the club in a descending arc. It means not quitting, but having in reserve another 50 percent of your force for coming through with a through-and-up swing that drives the ball long and accurately.

Remember to conserve 50 percent of your force for the up and through swing—but I don't mean to swing too hard or too fast or put too much of the lower gear into the swing. Think of the swing with the fairway wood just as you would think of the swing from a fairway with a short iron like the 9: It is an arms-and-hands-and-shoulders swing, the upper gear playing the leading role. The lower gear—hips and knees— plays the roles of supporting actors. And the star of the show, leading everyone else through the parade of the swing, is the club. As we shall see in tomorrow's lesson.

The key to swinging the fairway wood: meshing the downswing with the through swing. Put half the force into the downswing, but have in reserve another 50 percent of your force for the through-and-up swing that gets distance and accuracy.

Swing the club by moving only the upper gear—and you hear a whiz.

Practice: To prove to yourself that the upper gear is the dominant gear—and to impress your muscle memory with that fact of golfing life—swing the clubhead by grasping its neck and swinging the butt end with the left arm only—up, down, and through. You hear a *whiz*. That's the result of left-arm response, and that's the feeling you should get swinging a fairway wood—of the club swinging the body, not the body swinging the club. Now swing the club by moving only the shoulders and hips, the big muscles of your body. No *whiz*. Now swing the club by moving only the lower gear—hips, knees, and feet—while keeping the left arm and the club rigid. Again, no *whiz*. And again, proof positive that it's the upper gear who is the boss.

DAY 12

Long Irons: The Clubhead Leads the Parade

The long irons are the 1, 2, 3, and 4 irons. But I suggest you keep the 1 and 2 irons out of your bag. The 1 iron is strictly for advanced players. The 2 iron's long shaft and relatively little loft makes the club difficult for most weekenders to control. Use only the 3 and 4 irons.

For the long-iron shot, the ball is positioned in the center of the stance. (The exception would be if you were using a long iron to hit from the tee of a par-3 hole; then you would position the ball off the front heel.)

Your stance is square—that is, the toes are lined up on a line that is parallel to the line between the ball and the target. When you swing the long irons, the arc of the upswing and the arc of the downswing are wider than for shorter irons. That means there is more time for the body to sway. And if the body sways, throwing the path of the clubhead out of its proper arc, the clubhead will impact the ball with its face turned in or out.

You know what happens next. If the clubface is turned in toward you, the ball will hook to the left. If the clubface is turned out away from you, the ball will slice to the right. And since the clubface of the long irons is straighter than that for more lofted clubs, the ball is going to go a long way while it

The arc of the swing for the long irons, like the one in Walter's right hand, is wider—and thus takes longer to complete—than the arc for a short iron, like the one in his left hand.

is hook-spinning or slice-spinning. Also, the straight face will impart a lot more spin than will be imparted by a more lofted club. What this all adds up to: When you sway slightly while hitting with the long irons and bring the clubhead into the ball at even the slightest glancing angle toward you or away from you, the result is magnified by the club's straight face. A mistake with the long irons on even the widest fairway can send a ball slicing or hooking out of bounds.

Therefore, the foundation for the swing with the long irons is especially important. You must establish a solid base. Put a little more weight than usual on the back of the heels, pushing down into more of a sitting position. You don't want any toe dancing here. There is no lifting of the left heel on the upswing, especially for this shot.

Remind yourself, as you take your practice swings, that while the long irons are supposed to eat up distance, there is no need to swing hard and fast. Let the straight face do its work. Take an easy, controlled upswing—the same basic one for all shots. Allow the turning of the hips, knees, and shoulders to occur. End the upswing, as always, with the hands, arms, and club above the shoulders, your left shoulder touching your chin.

Start the downswing by again reminding yourself that there is no need to pulverize the ball. Rather, get the feeling that the hips and legs are giving you a solid foundation for a solid contact.

It is important, as I have just said, not to sway on the downswing. But, most important when swinging the long irons, don't ease up after impact. You hear that solid *click* and there is a temptation to think that the job is done. But you must continue your swing with your left arm extended straight out toward the target. The left arm is the connecting rod between the ball and your target.

As the through swing begins just after impact, the hips and knees must—I repeat, *must*—stay in the same position, facing the ball's original position, that they faced at address and at impact.

Let me explain why it is so important on long irons for the straight left arm to continue past the left leg—toward the

Hips and knees must not move, facing straight ahead until after the arms and clubhead have swept past the left leg toward the shaking-hands position.

shaking-hands position—while the body stays in place. This is the secret for hitting the long irons straight and long.

The longer-shafted irons make a longer arc on the downswing, as I said earlier, and a longer arc on the through swing. A longer arc takes longer to complete. It is going to take a longer time for the long iron's clubhead to travel from impact to the straight left-arm position in the through swing than it would take for a short iron to travel the same route.

It is vital, therefore, during the time that the clubhead moves from impact toward the connecting-rod position, that the hips and knees continue to face straight ahead.

Why? You probably have already realized why. If the hips and knees and shoulders turn to the left too soon after impact, they will turn the straight left arm to the left. And the ball will fly off to the left.

With a shorter iron, there is a shorter arc. It takes less time for the clubhead to go past the left side of the body. The body can come around almost instantly after impact.

But that's not so with the long irons, with their longer arc. The rest of the body—the knees, hips, and shoulders—must be patient. They must maintain a solid foundation until after impact. The body must wait for the clubhead to bring it around. The body can't jump the gun and move so fast that it brings the clubhead around.

This needs repeating: You must allow the clubhead to clear the left side. Only then do your knees and hips and shoulders come around. At impact and after impact, the knees and hips are behind the clubhead. The clubhead comes through first, and then knees and hips and the rest of the body follow.

Memorize this: *Your body doesn't bring the clubhead around. The clubhead brings the body around.*

Some weekenders try to give their long-iron shots a little extra *oomph.* They throw the right side of their body into the swing too soon after impact. Often, they will even lift up on their back foot too soon to put more body weight into their swing.

That's wrong for all shots. On every golf swing, the clubhead brings the body around. The clubhead comes first, and the shoulders, hips, and knees follow. But this is especially

The knees and hips come around to face the target during the follow-through. The clubhead leads the parade, and the hips and knees and the rest of the body follow.

important for the long irons because of the time required for the swing's longer arc.

As a final reminder to yourself, consider the pieces of the swing a parade. The clubhead leads the parade. The shoulders, hips, and knees—the rest of the body—come second in the parade.

Practice: Swing a long iron with the left hand only, swatting at a tee. Swinging the club in slow motion, make sure that as you bring the club into the impact area, the knees are pointing straight at the tee. Then, still swinging slowly, let the clubhead clear the left side before you turn the shoulders, hips, and knees. Increase the pace of the swing, getting the feeling of the clubhead leading the body around.

DAY 13

Middle Irons: The Confidence Builders

The swing with the middle irons—that is, the 5 and 6 irons—is the truest swing of all the golf-club swings: It is up at a slow pace, down at exactly the same pace, through at the same pace. It is a perfectly pure seesaw motion: The downswing and

1   2

the through swing match perfectly the upswing in tempo and pace. When I practice, I like to swing my 5 iron or my 6 iron, because I come closest when swinging with those two clubs to the feeling I want to have when I swing all my clubs. Consciously or unconsciously, most weekenders are most comfortable swinging the 5 iron or the 6 iron: The shafts, just right in length, allow that rolling rhythm that is a pure golf swing.

But make no mistake: You take a full golf swing with the middle irons. The club must come above the shoulders on the upswing, and the club must finish above the shoulders on the through swing. You are not trying to send the ball a great distance with the middle irons—150 yards is just about perfect—but there must be a full swing so that you get both the height you want with a middle iron and you get the accuracy you want with a middle iron. On short par 4s—those holes that are the easiest for weekenders to par or even birdie—you will be shooting for the green with a middle iron. You want the ball to land square onto the green from where you can putt for par or a birdie.

3

The swing with the middle irons is a perfectly pure seesaw motion: Left shoulder touches the chin on the upswing, right shoulder touches the chin on the downswing, and the follow-through is at the same pace as the upswing and the downswing.

Let me highlight the swing for the middle irons.

1. You use the same square stance you would use for all the clubs we have discussed. The ball is centered in the middle of your shoulder-width stance if the ball is on the fairway—that is, not teed up.
2. On the turn of the left side, the club comes up above the shoulders with a nice, easy tempo—think S-L-O-W.
3. The downswing must be exactly the same pace as the upswing. If you went up at 30 miles an hour, come down at 30 miles an hour. You want to make solid contact with the ball, but you don't apply any extra force.
4. If the tempo on the downswing is nice and slow, you can feel the clubhead getting ahead of the grip as both arms straighten to form the V just before impact. As the clubhead gets ahead of the grip (when the right shoulder drops below the left), the wrists are now straight for the important late release. This is a medium-iron shot, and medium means exactly that: a medium pace for medium distance. But you will get your 140 or more yards with these clubs—even with that medium 30-mile-an-hour pace—because the tempo of the swing will make the straightening of the wrists much easier as the right shoulder drops below the left. It's that straightening of the wrists—the "late hit"—that is, of course, the secret for distance in every shot.
5. You follow through at the same pace as the upswing and the downswing. Since the target is probably not a huge space of fairway, as it would be for the longer clubs, but perhaps a green only 20 yards wide, you must keep the left arm (the connecting rod) nice and straight until the clubhead has passed the beltline during the full and wide through swing. The clubhead and hands finish above the shoulders.

I call the middle irons the "confidence builders." After you have hit a series of stray shots with long irons or woods, pick up a 5 or 6 iron and remind yourself to go back to the pure golf swing—up, down, and through—the up and down and through each at the same pace. Thirty-five miles an hour up, 35 miles an hour down, 35 miles an hour through. You'll hit a decent, straight golf shot—and *presto!*—there's that old confidence back again.

Think tempo and think straight: The tempo is a take-it-easy tempo coming up, it is the same tempo coming down, it is the same tempo going through. The arms are straight just before and just after impact, and the arms are straight coming through.

Practice: To get that feeling of a swing that is equally matched in tempo, hold an imaginary club in your hands. Swing the club at an imaginary ball, matching the pace of the downswing and the through swing with the pace of the full upswing. Then take a 5 or 6 iron and swing the club at an imaginary ball. Since the club shaft is not long, you can relate easily to the feeling you had when you swung only with your hands and the feeling you now have swinging with the club.

Finally, take two or three swings at a ball, again trying to get the same feeling you felt when you swung with only your hands. Go back and repeat the process: Swing only with the hands, then only with the club, and finally take two or three swings with the club at a ball.

Get that feeling of rolling to the right on the upswing, and rolling to the left on the downswing and the through swing.

Up, down, through. And swing. Don't hit.

DAY 14

The Short Irons: Your Scoring Clubs

Occasionally, you may shoot for a green with a middle iron, but not often. Most weekenders stand too far away from the green to hit it with their second shot on a par-4 hole, or to land on the green with their third shot on a par-5 hole. Most will stand within 100 yards of the green for their third shot on a par-4 hole. Most will stand within 100 yards of the green for their fourth shot on a par-5 hole. It's from there that they pull out one of their short irons—a 7 iron from about 120 yards away, an 8 iron from about 110 yards away, a 9 iron from about 100, and a pitching wedge from within 80 yards.

That's why I call the short irons your scoring irons. These are the clubs you hit to a green for a two-putt green. Or, if there is no trap in your way, you can aim for the pin and hope to one-putt.

But most weekenders hit short to a green with their short irons. As any teaching pro will tell you, if there is one cardinal sin that keeps weekenders out of below-100 heaven, it is that "they come up short of the green." (The second cardinal sin, the pros will tell you, is that weekenders also come up short too often on their putts.)

Let's look first at what weekenders do wrong and what causes them to land short with their approach shots. Then we'll look at what you should be doing right—the things that could save you perhaps a half-dozen strokes a round.

Wrong! *Throwing the right side of the body into the swing with the short irons, to scoop the ball upward, may produce height, but the mistake will cost distance and accuracy.*

Weekenders have been told, "You've got to hit down on the ball to get it up." But they are afraid to hit down. It doesn't make sense to them. What makes sense to them: Scooping *up* the ball. At first glance, that seems to make sense: Scooping up seems more logical than hitting down if you want the ball to go up.

So what the weekender does is this: He or she throws the right side of the body—knees, hips, and shoulders—into the swing. The golfer brings the right side of the body around ahead of the clubhead. The weight of the body acts as the force that literally shovels or scoops the ball upward.

Often, they do get height. But two bad things happen with this scooping action. First, the right shoulder comes around in front of the left shoulder. That throws the ball to the left of the target.

Secondly, while this action does produce height, the weekender pays dearly for that altitude. Since the body brings the clubhead around—instead of the clubhead bringing the body around—there is no great clubhead speed. And there is no full follow-through, because the body's weight is ahead of the clubhead instead of being where it belongs—behind the clubhead.

Impact and follow-through are weak. Result: No "send" to the ball—and it drops short.

What happens next, of course, is that the weekender must take another short iron and hit a second shot to get to the green he should have reached in one stroke, not two strokes. Do that four or five times in a round—and I have seen weekenders land short on each par-4 and par-5 hole they played—and you have tacked on at least a half-dozen needless strokes.

Hit down to get the ball up. This is especially true with the short irons. You must trust a sharply descending blow—and the high degree of loft on the short irons' clubface—to get the ball up.

Let's highlight what you must remember when swinging the short irons:

As with all clubs, the stance is square, the ball in the middle of the stance.

The spine is inclined at about the same angle that you

would bend when hitting a drive off the tee. But since these are the shortest-shafted clubs, you must bend to reach the ball. But you bend more at the knees, sitting down a little more, not at the waist.

On the downswing, the clubhead travels a shorter distance to impact the ball than it travels for any other club. The reason is obvious: The radius of the swing with a long-shafted club, like a driver, is longer—and thus travels a longer distance—than the radius of the short irons.

Therefore—and listen carefully, now—it is important that the downswing be as moderate and equal in speed as the upswing. This is even more important with the short irons than with the medium irons. The swing arc is so short in distance that you may not give yourself the time to sequence each part of the swing in its proper order. So take your time to make sure that:

1. The downswing is more sharply angled than the downswing with any other club. This steeply sloped swing will allow the lofted clubface to catch the bottom of the ball and then continue downward so that the clubface slices an arc-shaped sliver of ground—the divot. The lofted clubface sends the ball upward at a steep angle.
2. Just before impact, the wrists straighten (or uncock) when the right shoulder has dropped below the left. The clubhead comes ahead of the club's grip. This is the "late hit" that will add distance to your shot and not leave you short.
3. Your right shoulder, as it drops under your chin after impact, stays on the same line with the left shoulder (a line that is parallel to the line from ball to target). If the left shoulder swings out in front of the right shoulder, you are going to hit the ball off line, probably to the left.
4. The left arm stays straight after impact and into the bottom half of the through swing. That straight arm is the connecting rod between the ball and the target.

Remember that the sharp descending blow and the loft on the clubface get the ball up into the air. The straight left arm in the through swing directs the ball to the target. The full and wide through swing gives the ball its "send" so that it goes the distance to your target.

Here's another reason why weekenders hit short on their short-iron approach shots: When their clubhead hits the ground to take the divot, there is a tendency to slow up or stop the swing. Result: There is only a halfhearted through swing. It is a "stab" shot—and the ball doesn't go very far. You may end up in a trap and need three or four strokes to go the distance you should have gone in one stroke. Go through the divot and take a full and wide through swing, the clubhead and hands ending above your shoulders.

A final word about the divot. The divot should start about a half-inch to an inch on the left side of the ball's original position. If you see that your divots are starting on the right of the ball's original position, you are hitting what we call a "fat" shot. That means you are hitting the ground first, then the ball—and what you produce is a fattie that nearly always lumbers short of your target. Check your divots to make sure they start out to the left—or the target side—of where the ball sat.

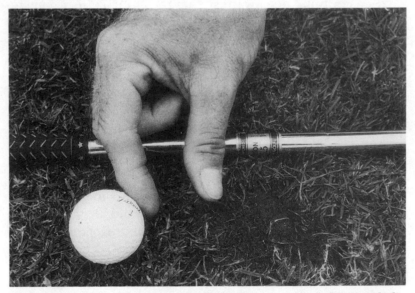

The divot should start a half-inch to an inch to the left, or target side, of the ball's original position.

Practice: To make sure you are hitting the ball first and then the ground, place a tee in the middle of your stance. Place another tee, also in the middle of the stance but a foot away from you so you can't hit it. Swing at the first tee with a short iron. Check where your divot begins by comparing the divot's position to the second tee. The divot should begin about a half-inch to the left of the tee. Then your swing is contacting the ball first, then the ground, and you will be getting the distance you want.

Here's another way to practice coming through a divot to finish with a full follow-through. Go to a lawn or vacant lot where the grass has grown three or four inches high. Place an imaginary ball in the middle of your stance. Swing at the imaginary ball so that you shear the grass to the ground level two or three inches in front of the ball's position and two or three inches behind the ball's position. This drill will help you to erase the tendency to "stab"—that is, to stop or slow down the club after contacting the ground. Teach yourself to bring the clubhead through the catching action created by divots.

DAY 15

Reading the Green: The Key to Sinking Second Putts

You start to read greens—just as you start on the road to a below-100 round—at the practice green. Don't skip the practice green in your eagerness to tee off. More than 40 percent of your strokes will be taken on greens. If you are serious about breaking 100, you must give at least 15 minutes to warming up your putting stroke before a round.

Three or four putts at the practice green should tell you whether the other greens on the course are fast, slow, or normal. On most courses, the practice green is a true barometer of what the rest of the greens are like.

Now, let's define a term here: What does reading a green include? Basically, these two things:

1. How fast or how slow the putt will roll.
2. In what direction the ball will roll—straight to the hole or to the left or right.

Let's go to the first green, where we are looking at a 20-foot putt. Stand a few feet behind the ball and look at the line from ball to cup. Some golfers like to crouch low as they look at the line. But I think that if you stand tall, you will see much more clearly any hills or valleys the ball must roll up or down on its way to the cup.

Is your putt going straight uphill? Stroke the putt more firmly than normal. Is the putt going straight downhill? Use a softer touch.

At the practice green, you got a reading on the speed of the green. You can confirm what you learned by "going to school" here on the first green. Watch the putts of the other players before you putt. The speed of their putts will tell you the speed of the green. Observe whether the green has been recently cut; a recent mowing will almost certainly indicate a faster green than normal. Recent rain or morning dew will soften a green and make it slower than normal.

Now, what about direction? Is your putt going straight uphill? In this case, a firmer putt than normal for this distance will be needed. Is the ball going straight downhill? If so, a softer touch than normal will be needed.

Now, let me make two points here.

1. Whether you are putting uphill with firmness or downhill with a soft touch, keep in mind that the mechanics of all putts are the same. We take the club back a certain distance, we come through to hit the ball with the clubface square, and the follow-through is equal in distance to the takeaway. The mechanics stay the same; what changes is the length of the takeaway and follow-through, and the force applied at impact.

2. Most pros will tell you that an uphill putt is usually easier than a downhill. When you putt uphill, you know that even if you swing too hard, the ball—going uphill—will probably not roll too far past the cup. But you get a scary feeling putting downhill. If you putt too hard, the ball could roll downhill to the other end of the green, leaving you at least two putts to hole out. So, when you pitch and run from the apron to the cup, or when you are stroking a long putt, try to leave your next putt an uphill one rather than a downhill one. In short, think next putt.

Back on that first green, suppose we see that the cup is cut into the side of a slope. As the ball slows down near the hole, the slope will drag the ball from right to left down the slope and away from the hole. How do we make the ball break toward the hole?

On putts that break, aim for an imaginary hole (the large ball) at the point where you want the ball to slow down. You then use gravity—that is, the slope of the green—to carry the ball to the real hole.

I ask myself: As the ball slows down near the cup, how many inches will the slope drag the ball downward to the left and away from the cup? Looking at the angle of the slope, I get my answer: four inches. That's just about the width of one cup.

Now I "borrow" four inches from the green. I aim for an imaginary hole about four inches (one cup) to the right of the real cup. As the ball slows down as it approaches the imaginary cup, it should break right to left, rolling down the slope and into the hole.

I aim for that imaginary hole on all breaking putts except those within two feet of the cup. Then I ignore the break. I hit the ball so firmly, aiming for that imaginary "backboard" I told you about on day 8, that the ball rolls right through the slope, going so fast that gravity can't drag it down the slope.

Many pros will tell you that, when reading a green, you should aim the putt so that it goes past the hole rather than stopping short of the hole. The ball can't go in if it doesn't get to the hole. *Never up, never in!* In most cases, I would agree. But if you see that putting long will leave you a tricky return putt, you may be better off leaving the putt short. Again: Think next putt.

Being able to read a green won't let you sink 20 long putts in a row. But what it will do is help to get you close enough to sink a lot more second putts—the big key to breaking 100.

DAY 16

Coming Back From Trouble—In Only One Stroke!

Two things happen to many weekenders when they land in trouble—in trees, a rough, or a fairway bunker. Each of the two things can cost you extra strokes.

1. You get down on yourself. *You'll never be any good at this game. Who needs this frustration?* Gone is your concentration, gone are your chances of breaking 100.
2. You get fired up. *OK, I hit a bad shot, but I'll zoom this next shot to that green.* You try to force the shot, and you end up in deeper trouble. Now, instead of one mistake costing you one stroke, two mistakes will cost you two strokes—at least.

Let this be your first rule for hitting out of trouble: Accept the one stroke that the trouble cost you. Hit the ball back to the nearest part of the fairway and start all over again. If you can hit toward the green and advance the ball, fine. But if your safest route back to the fairway means you have to hit the ball sideways or backwards, hit the ball sideways or backwards.

In short, when in trouble, think first about hitting to safety.

Now, having said that, let me add this: At times, when in a rough, trees, or the sand of a fairway bunker, you can be bold.

If your ball lands high in the rough (left), you can use a wood. But if it is half or fully buried (right), use a lofted iron.

You can scramble to get the seemingly impossible par or bogey.

Here is how to get out of the three most common trouble spots with one stroke:

ROUGH

You can land in a rough where the grass is above your knee-caps, and you can land in rough where the grass is no higher than your shoetops. If the ball lands in low rough and is sitting on top of the grass, just as it would sit for a fairway shot, you can play the ball as you would play any ball on the fairway from this distance—with a wood or an iron. Stance and swing are the same.

If the rough is above your shoes, you might be lucky and find your ball sitting on top of a mound of grass, looking teed up. Make good use of your luck. Take out a wood, if the distance calls for it, and swing the wood as you would hit a ball off a tee—that is, the ball up front opposite the left heel.

More often than not, however, the ball is buried in medium to deep rough. It is impossible to get the face of a wood into that much grass; the grass will catch the clubface and cause it to open or turn at impact, and you will slice or hook if you even get the ball airborne. There is a temptation to take a highly lofted wood, like a 7, and try to force the ball out with the impact of an extra-powerful swing.

Resist the temptation. The club just doesn't have the tools needed to do the job.

Go to a 6 or 7 iron and aim to pitch the ball to the nearest stretch of fairway. (In deep rough, the strongest club I would choose would be a 5 iron.) The swing is different than for a fairway shot. The upswing and downswing are steeply angled, so you catch as little grass as possible. The grass can slow the swing; it can also turn the clubface. Give as much as 75 percent of your energy to the downswing, the remaining 25 percent to the through swing—not the usual 50%-50%. You want to shatter that grass, shear right through it as though the club were a scythe, catching the bottom of the ball and arching it toward the general area of the fairway. Remember: Accuracy is not as important on this shot as getting the ball airborne quickly. Nor is distance important—you want to go only to the nearest part of the fairway. But since grass will be sandwiched between the clubface and the ball, there will be no backspin and you will get a lot of roll. That may be helpful—but just know that it is likely to happen. Don't aim the ball toward a bunker that a "flyer," as we call shots like these, may reach.

FAIRWAY BUNKER

Most fairway bunkers are long and shallow, and since balls usually roll into them, the ball is often sitting on top of the sand. If the ball is sitting up high, you can be bold and try to gobble up the distance you would gobble up with a fairway shot. But if the ball is half buried in the sand, blast it out to

Position the ball for the fairway-bunker shot so that the clubhead catches the ball while the clubhead is coming through the bottom of the swing—not while the club is descending, as you do for a fairway shot. The smudge in the sand in the center of Walter's stance is where the ball is positioned for a fairway shot. The smudge opposite Walter's front toe is where he has positioned the ball—and contacted it—for the fairway-bunker shot.

the fairway as you would blast a ball from a greenside bunker. Then go for distance.

But let's assume you have a good lie. Here are the keys to a successful shot from a fairway bunker:

1. Size up the distance to your target. If you figure you would need a 7 iron from this distance, use a 6 iron instead. You want a stronger club. If the clubhead nicks the sand at all before it hits the ball, you will lose clubhead speed—and distance. The stronger club can make up for distance lost if you do catch some sand before impact.
2. Standing at the address position, shuffle your feet into the sand. You don't want to stand *on* the sand, you want to stand *in* the sand. You need a solid foundation, because if your body moves you will impact sand and you'll be lucky if the ball moves three feet.
3. Position the ball off the front foot. You want to try to catch the ball on the upswing when the club is moving away from the sand.
4. The swing is dominated by the upper gear—hands, arms, shoulders, and club. You use the lower gear only a little— the knees move slightly—while keeping your hips and knees on hold. That minimizes the chances of body movement.
5. The pace of the swing should be very slow. Don't let the sand make you think you have to whack that ball hard to set it free. Take an easy swing, with only the hands and arms and shoulders, concentrating on meeting the ball cleanly and following through with the left arm straight until it reaches the belt buckle. Finish with hands and club-head high above the shoulders.

TREES

This is no time to be bold. This is a time to look for the widest opening between the trees and aim your shot to go through that opening. If that opening is at a place where you must shoot 180 degrees away from the green, so be it.

1   2

The punch shot is the shot I prescribe for getting out of the woods.

To make the punch shot, use a strong club like the 3 or 4 iron. Its straight face will keep the ball low and also allow it to run a good distance after it lands.

The stance is narrow, feet close together and close to the ball. On the upswing, bring back the hands only waist high, the clubshaft only slightly above the waist, the wrists hinging only slightly.

On both the backswing and the downswing, there is no body movement that might cause the clubface to turn in or out at impact. Only the arms and hands move. There is only a slight movement in toward the ball with the left knee on the upswing, a slight movement of the right knee in toward the ball on the downswing. Other than that, there is no body movement that might cause the clubface to turn in or out at impact. You want to impact the ball with the same straight face that you addressed the ball with. This ball must go straight as an arrow between the trees.

On the downswing, concentrate on striking the bottom of

The punch shot out of trees. On the upswing, bring the hands up only waist high, the wrists hinging only slightly. On the downswing, concentrate on striking the bottom of the ball. Stop the through swing when the hands get waist high.

3

the ball. There should be a firm straightening of the wrists as the clubhead moves in front of the club's grip. Stop the through swing as the hands get waist high. You don't want a full follow-through that will get the ball too high into the air. It should ride no more than ten feet high and leave you on the fairway.

I call this kind of shot a comeback shot, whether it's from a bunker, trees, or rough. When you get into trouble, come back—at the least cost in strokes—to where you can get your game going again.

DAY *17*

Club Selection and Course Strategy: Let One Stroke Do the Work of Two!

Most above-100 golfers land their approach shots short of the green. When you stand about 100 yards away from a green and you drop your approach shot short of the green, you are taking two strokes to cover the distance you should have covered in one stroke—and that's positively perilous to your chances of breaking 100.

Landing short of a green, I have observed, is often—if not always—caused by 1) poor club selection; and 2) faulty course strategy.

CLUB SELECTION

Know thyself! That's the key to clubbing. Start knowing thyself, golf-wise, by going to a driving range that has a 150-yard marker or to any open field where you can pace off 150 yards. (One normal stride equals a yard.) Swing at a dozen or more golf balls with a 5 iron, aiming for that 150-yard marker. Did most of your shots drop short of the 150-yard marker? Switch to a 4 iron. Aim another dozen balls to that 150-yard target. Did most of the shots reach 150 yards? Make a note of how many balls land close to 150 yards with the 4 iron. The next day, again swing at about a dozen or so balls, aiming to reach that 150-yard spot with the 4 iron. If, again, most of your shots land 150 yards away, you can be reasonably certain that your standard club for 150 yards is the 4 iron.

Whatever club you find is your standard for 150 yards, you can make your own club-selection chart based on this one for our golfer who hits 150 yards with the 4 iron:

CLUB	DISTANCE
3 iron or 4 or 5 wood	157 or more yards
4 iron or 6 or 7 wood	150 to 156 yards
5 iron	142 to 149 yards
6 iron	134 to 141 yards
7 iron	126 to 133 yards
8 iron	118 to 125 yards
9 iron	110 to 117 yards
Pitching wedge	Within 110 yards

As you can see, the rule of thumb is 7. Go one club stronger than your standard for each 7 yards beyond 150 yards, go one club less for each 7 yards shorter than 150 yards.

There are three caveats to this chart:

1. If the wind is blowing from behind your back, choose one club less—a 6 iron instead of a 5 iron, for example—than the one you would normally use for a given distance. If the wind is blowing in your face or blowing across the fairway, choose one club stronger—a 4 instead of a 5, for example.

2. When in doubt, always go to the stronger club. On most holes, trouble sits usually in front of a green, less often behind the green. More often than not, whether you are shooting for a green or any other target, you are in a better position for your next shot when you hit long rather than short.

3. When in rough and hitting with an iron, remember that grass, sandwiched between the clubface and the ball, will

reduce or eliminate any backspin. The ball will roll when it lands. Choose one club higher than normal for this distance—a 7 instead of a 6, for example.

COURSE STRATEGY

Each hole on a golf course calls for a strategy of its own. But there are basic guidelines for all holes. I have three basic ones:

1. Bogeys are good—and double bogeys are OK, too.

Remember that par—it's 72 on most courses—is a number for people like Nicklaus and Watson to worry about. You are playing bogey golf. If you bogey every hole, you will come in 18 strokes above par—a 90. Now, that would not send you home in tears, would it?

Keep this also in mind: If you bogied ten holes and if you double-bogeyed the other eight holes, that adds up this way: 16 strokes over par for the eight holes you double-bogeyed and ten strokes over par for the ten holes you bogeyed.

You know what 10 + 16 equals. It comes to 26. And 72 plus 26 equals 98. Scoring a 98 is what this book is all about.

2. Aim for the safety valve.

Your target, when you stand at a tee, is not the green on any hole except a par 3—and often the green should not be your target even on a par 3. Your target should be the safest and best area from which you will launch your next shot. In short, before every shot, you should be thinking: "Where do I want to be when I take my next shot?"

3. Make the critical shot on each hole your most comfortable shot.

The critical shot on each hole is the shot that you must land on the green to get a chance at your bogey or your double bogey. What is that critical shot for each hole?

On a par-3 hole, the critical shot is usually your second shot. On a par-4 hole, the critical shot is your third shot. On a par-5 hole, the critical shot is the fourth shot. Let's play a typical par 3, a typical par 4, and a typical par 5 for our lessons over the next three days, and I will show you how to make each hole's most critical shot your most comfortable, pressure-free shot.

DAY *18*

Playing the Par 3s: Making the Most Demanding Shot a Comfort Shot

Many golfers welcome par-3 holes as easy holes. Some short par 3s, 120 yards or so, are relatively easy. But on a par-3 hole of 150 or more yards, your tee shot is the most demanding shot in all of golf.

I am sure you know why. You must try to land that tee shot on a small target—the green—to two-putt and save your par 3. But traps usually lurk in front of those par-3 greens—frontal traps like the ones on this 180-yard par 3 at my home course at the Hempstead Golf and Country Club. And those traps sometimes seem to have arms and teeth to grab anything flying by.

Your critical shot on a par 3 can be your first or your second shot. On this particular hole, you can go for the green on the tee shot if you have been playing well all day and there is no wind blowing in your face.

But aim for a safety-valve zone. On this hole, that would be the right side of the green just beyond the trap, which is out about 160 yards. If you think you can carry that trap with a 3 or 4 wood, go for the right side where there is no trouble. Don't swing the driver, because your shot must be straight

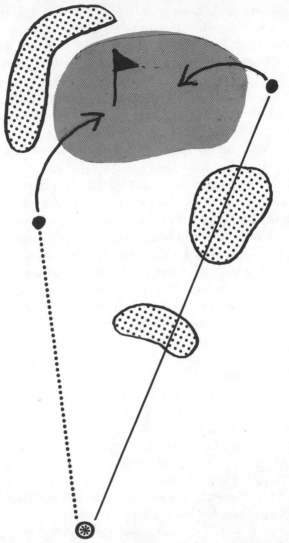

On this 180-yard par 3, aim for the right side of the
green if you have been hitting well. Your second shot
would then put you close to the pin. But the safer way
to play a par 3 is to aim for a safety-valve area like the
left side of this fairway. Your critical second shot will
be a comfortable one. You'll be swinging a favorite
club like the 6 or 7 iron from a short distance of no
more than 50 yards.

and the driver allows no margin for error if you impact the ball with even the slightest kind of glancing blow.

A 180-yard drive to the right side of the green, even if you slice slightly and end up off the green, will leave you with a long putt or a pitch-and-roll shot for a par 3 or bogey 4, which is par as far as you are concerned.

A tip when going for a green on par-3 holes: Think long. Aim for beyond the pin. On most holes, as I have said, the trouble usually sits in front of the green. If you drive over the green, you usually face only a short pitch or a chip to get back. And if you mis-hit and don't get all the club into the ball, you will land short, of course, but short drops you onto the green. So when aiming for a green on a par-3 hole, choose one club stronger than you would usually use for this distance. Take a nice, easy swing so you let the club do the work—not the force of your swing—and if you land long, that's nearly always better on any hole than landing short.

Now, let's be more conservative in our course strategy. If the wind is blowing into your face, or if you are hitting poorly, *or* if you just want to be safe instead of sorry, I would suggest this: Make your second shot the critical shot while also making it your easiest shot.

Take a 6 or 7 wood or a 4 or 5 iron—your most comfortable club—and aim for the left of the fairway about 120 to 150 yards away. That's a safety-valve area where there is no trouble. Take a nice, easy, cruising swing and just lay it out there well short of the green and the traps.

Now, standing from 30 to 50 yards from the green, you face nothing but that wide green for your second shot. Pitching with a 7 iron from this short distance, you can aim for the pin. A decent shot will land you close enough for two putts and a "par" 4, while a perfect pitch can get you a "birdie" 3. And you reached the green for that 3 or 4 with two easy, comfortable, pressure-free shots.

DAY 19

Playing the Par 4s: Why Misfortune Need Not Cost You "Par"

This 408-yard par 4 at Hempstead is not a long hole. But I want to play it with you to demonstrate that even on the short par 4s, it is the third shot—not the first or second—that you should make both your most important shot and your easiest shot.

Certainly, you are not going to reach the green from the tee. On all par 4s and par 5s, think in these terms: My tee shot should stay on the fairway and gobble up some distance. But it should never be a Sunday-blast kind of shot whose force causes you to mis-hit, slicing or hooking out of bounds (costing you two strokes).

From the tee you can't reach the trap out on the right about 230 yards. Let's take a slow and steady swing with the driver—up, down, and through—that will travel 150 to 175 yards and stay on the fairway.

Few things work perfectly in golf, and this tee shot is among those things that go agley. You hit far enough, about 170 yards, but you slice off to the right and end up embedded in thick rough.

No panic. You take a 5 or 6 iron, whichever is your most comfortable club. You tell yourself you want to lob the ball back into the fairway and advance the ball as far as you can.

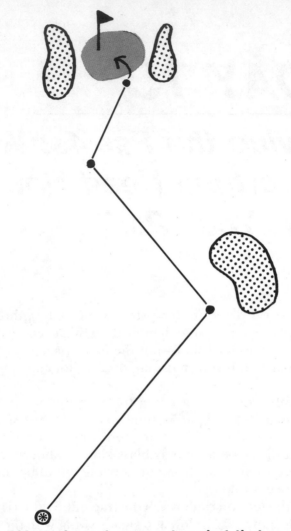

On this 408-yard par 4, even a tee shot that goes too far to the right and lands in the rough won't destroy your chances for a bogey 5. An iron shot out of the rough and an approach shot that falls short means you lie 3. A pitch-and-roll to the pin and a short putt will give you a 5 that you had to scramble for. But your critical third shot on this par 4 was a comfortable one.

But your first thought is getting to the safety of the fairway.

You aim for the traps fronting the green on the left, knowing you will not reach them. Taking a comfortable swing, you pitch to the left side and come down about 120 yards away. You now stand about 100 yards from the green.

For your critical third shot, you pick a 9 or a pitching wedge, whichever you like better. You hold the club firmly; you'll take a divot and you don't want the club to jar out of your grip as it goes through the ground. Again, an easy up, down, and through swing, with a full follow-through.

Good news and bad news. The bad news: You hit "fat," behind the ball, and the shot lands short on the rim of the green. The good news: The ball sits smack in front of the pin that's 30 feet away.

You take a 7 iron for your pitch-and-run. You aim for a spot midway between the ball and the pin. You pitch-and-run to within two feet of the cup. You roll in the putt for your bogey, a par to you.

There was no pressure on you for that critical third shot. On all four shots to the green, you never had to swing all-out—and risk a mis-hit. It is the mis-hits, more often than not, that the hazards catch.

DAY 20

Playing the Par 5s: Where You Can Be the Equal of the Long Hitters

These are the holes that sorely test your determination to swing easy. When you are standing on the tee of a 550-yard hole, driver in hand, that green looks a county and a half away. There is a powerful urge to blast that ball off the tee with a swing that kills.

I tell my students, "Your most powerful tee shot—your best ever—plus the one or two best fairway-wood shots of your career, put together, will not land you on the green in two strokes. They probably won't put you onto the green in three strokes.

"Why not take three easy swings—what I call a cruisin' swing? After those three easy swings, you will stand within a hundred yards, maybe even fifty yards, of the green on the longest par five."

Now what, then, is your situation? You stand within a 9 iron or a pitching wedge of the green. Your partner, who has hit two long shots, also stands within 100 yards of the green, and he too holds a 9 iron or a pitching wedge in his hands.

Now, of course, not all of us can hit the ball 250 yards with

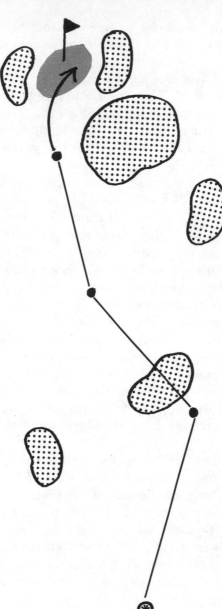

On this 510-yard par 5, three easy swings will bring you close to or within a hundred yards of the green—close enough so that the critical fourth shot is pressure-free.

our drivers. But we all can hit from 50 to 100 yards with the wedge. It is here, close to the green, that all golfers become equals.

That's why I call the par 5s, like this five hundred ten-yarder at Hempstead, The Great Equalizers. If you can land on the green with the wedge on your fourth shot while your long-hitting partner misses and lands short with his third shot, he must hit a fourth to get on the green and be even with you.

On this hole I would suggest you swing with your driver to get you out about 160 to 175 yards. Even if you slice into the rough on the right, you are all right. For your second shot, depending on your lie, hit a long iron or a 5 wood to eat up a decent amount of distance. Keep the ball on the fairway, which is wide enough to allow your shot to stray a little without leaving you in trouble.

Your third shot, taken with a medium iron or again with the 5 wood, will drop you from 100 to 120 yards of the green.

Now you can take one of your most comfortable clubs, perhaps a 5 or 6 iron. I would suggest one club stronger than you would normally use for this distance. You want to land on the green or behind the green. There are no problems behind the green, and there are certainly no problems being on the green. But if you land short, those frontal bunkers may catch you.

Here's another reason to hit with a stronger club than normal when you are aiming for a green: In your mind you will know you have the firepower to reach the green even if your swing doesn't catch all of the ball. And you know you don't have to throw your body or anything extra into the swing. There is no temptation to add a little extra zing to the swing—and mis-hit, producing a slice or hook that will leave you in trouble. Use an easy swing and trust the firepower within the club.

True, if you catch the ball perfectly, you will land at the far end of the green or even behind the green. But a good pitch-and-roll or a chip shot will get you close enough to the pin to hole out with one or two putts. Even if you land at the far end of the green and need three putts to hole out, a double-bogey 7 on a par-5 hole of this size still gives you plenty of room to break 100.

And most important, you made the fourth shot, that critical approach shot to the green, an easy shot. There was no pressure to hit especially long or especially accurately. *You could make a golf swing, not a golf hit.* In fact, all four shots to reach the green were free of pressure. And it is pressure, as any golfer from Bobby Jones to Greg Norman will tell you, that adds strokes to a score.

DAY 21

How the Rules Can Save You Strokes

Many weekenders try to break 100 by ignoring or making up the rules as they go along. Two notable examples that I have noticed: Sam hits a ball out of bounds. Sam drops a ball near where the ball went out of bounds. He takes a one-stroke penalty and hits his next shot, his third of the hole, to the target.

Wrong!

When you hit a ball out of bounds, you no longer have a ball in play. You must go back to where you hit the ball from, then swing again. You must take, in other words, both a one-stroke penalty and a distance penalty, so that you are now hitting three from where you took your first stroke.

Or Sam hits a ball into the woods and can't find it. Sam says, "I'll just drop a ball." He takes a one-stroke penalty and hits from about where he guesses the ball vanished.

Again, wrong!

You must go back and hit another ball from where you hit the first, taking both the stroke penalty and the distance penalty.

(To speed up play, when you think you have hit out of bounds or into a place where you might not be able to find the ball, hit a provisional ball. Then you can play the provisional ball if you can't find the first one.)

Let's break 100 honestly by obeying the rules. Better still, let's break 100 by taking advantage of the rules.

That means reading and knowing the rules (which are available in a book published by the United States Golf Association and Perigee Books, G. P. Putnam's Sons, and sold in bookstores). Let's look at three situations where knowing the rules could mean the difference between a 101 and a 99 or lower.

Free-drop situations

If you hit a ball into a place that does not usually exist on the course—a puddle of water left by a rainstorm, for example, or a hole dug by a dog or another burrowing animal—you can pick up the ball and drop it into a playable lie without penalty. You can drop the ball a club's length away in any direction except toward the green.

Pick the best spot to drop. For example, it certainly makes sense to drop the ball in the close-cropped fairway when that's only a club's length away, rather than into nearby wet and thick rough. And look to drop the ball so that you have an unobstructed line to the green.

Unplayable-lie Situations

Any golfer can rule on his own that his ball sits in an unplayable lie no matter where it rests on the course, except if it's in a water hazard (he should notify his partners of his ruling). If a ball sits under a tree, for example, he may deem the ball unplayable and take a one-stroke penalty for moving it.

Again, know where to drop the ball so you can profit the most from the one-stroke price that this is costing you. You are allowed to drop the ball two club's lengths from where the ball lies to the left or right or as far back as you would like to go. It would make no sense to drop the ball where the tree stands between you and the green. If you hit the tree again, you may pay another one-stroke penalty. Choose a spot from where you have the best line to your next target.

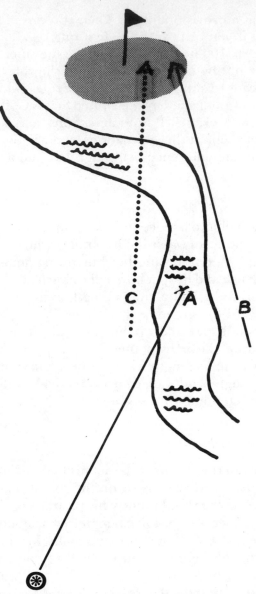

When your shot (A) lands in the water and you have an option where to drop the ball for your next shot, pick B, where you have a water-free line to the green, not C, where you must hit over more water.

Water-hazard situations

There are two kinds of water hazards—frontal and lateral. A frontal water hazard sits between you and your target. If you splash a ball into the water, you must drop another ball (at a cost of one stroke). You may have to drop the ball into a designated drop area, or you may be allowed to drop the ball along the same line that your ball was traveling when it hit the water. But you must drop the ball on the far side of the water, not the green side. Here it makes sense to drop the ball, when you can, so that you need to cover the shortest stretch of water to the green.

A lateral water hazard runs more or less parallel to the fairway. If you splash a ball into a lateral hazard, and if course rules allow, drop the ball where you have a line to the green with no water in between. Let's face it, hitting over even a little bit of water is a psychological hazard that costs strokes.

Obey the rules. Breaking or ignoring rules to score below 100 can give you no real sense of triumph. But know the rules so that they can give you back as many or more strokes as they take away.

The Day You Break 100

I can't be with you from here on out—unless you want to come back for refreshers from day 1 to day 21. I do suggest to all my students that they come back periodically for refreshers where I remind them: *This is a golf swing, not a golf hit.*

As you go out onto your home course to smash the 100 barrier, I would like to be at your ear whispering tips. Since that is impossible, I will do the next best thing. I will give you a basic checklist that you should keep with you. Copy it and stuff it into a pocket. Whenever your game goes sour, go over this checklist point by point. Chances are, you will find what's gone wrong so you can make it go right.

1. Make sure the grip is right: square on the left side, square on the right side, the palms facing each other. Make sure the V of the thumbs and forefingers point to the right shoulder.
2. Looking down at the clubface, is the clubface square to the line to the target?
3. Taking your stance, make sure the feet, knees, and hips are lined up on a line that is parallel to the target line.
4. At address, make sure that both arms are straight forming a V pattern.
5. Take a practice swing that is not just a casual swing but a clone in tempo of what will be your actual swing at the ball.
6. Make sure on your upswing that hands and club rise above the shoulders. The left shoulder must pass under the chin—not in front or across the chin. When the left shoulder touches the chin, that's the signal the upswing

is finished. The left knee must point in toward the ball, not straight ahead or behind the ball.

7. Take a moment's pause at the top of the swing—but not by coming to a complete halt.

8. As the clubhead comes down, you should feel that it is coming down almost at the same pace and force that you used to take the club up and away from the ball. As the clubhead comes down, the right knee must point in toward the ball—not behind the ball.

9. The most important part of the golf swing is to re-form—just before impact—the arms and wrists and hands into the V pattern that they formed at address.

10. As the clubhead enters the impact zone—and as the right shoulder drops below the left—the wrists straighten so the clubhead moves in front of the grip, creating that "snap" of the wrists that adds fire to the clubhead and zing to the shot.

11. After impact, make sure that the arms and hands clear the left thigh before the clubhead brings the right side of the body around.

12. Finish with the arms *wide and away from the body,* the hands up high—I can't stress that too much—so that they are high above the shoulders on the follow-through.

13. As you follow through, the clubhead is pulling the weight around from your right side so that you finish with the weight entirely on the left side and the body turned so that it is facing toward where the ball is going—not where the ball was. As you follow through, the right shoulder must drop below the left and must pass under the chin—not in front of the chin.

That's it—the lessons are over. You're being called to the first tee. That 100 barrier is sitting out there on the course defying you to smash it.

Smash it!

Left to right: Aime La Montagne, Walter Ostroske, John Devaney.

About the Authors

Walter Ostroske has been a PGA Teaching Pro for the past twenty-five years. He has played in numerous tournaments and has written magazine articles on golf instruction. Currently head pro at the Hempstead Golf and Country Club on Long Island, he is a member of the MacGregor Advisory Staff.

John Devaney is the author of more than twenty-five books and has written hundreds of magazine articles on sports. The former editor of *Sport Magazine,* he is the editor of Harris Publications golf magazines and is an adjunct lecturer at Fordham University.

Improve your game, find the reference material you need, and learn all the rules "officially," in these comprehensive Perigee golf guides.

The Whole Golf Catalog
by Rhonda Glenn and Robert R. McCord
illustrated with line drawings and photographs

The Whole Golf Catalog covers all aspects of golf with information for both the amateur and the professional. It includes lists of professional and amateur golf associations, golf museums and archives, and instructional golf camps and tours; sources of golf merchandise, publishers of golf books and magazines, games, and software; a calendar of important golf events; and much more! Packed with photos, line drawings, and up-to-date information, it is the standard reference for all golfers and golf fans.

Golf Rules in Pictures
An Official Publication of the United States Golf Association
Introduction by Arnold Palmer

Scores of clearly captioned pictures cover all the rules of golf: scoring, number of clubs allowed, procedure when a player's ball is hit accidentally, hazards, and penalty strokes. Included is the complete text of The Rules of Golf as approved by the United States Golf Association and the Royal and Ancient Golf Club of St. Andrews, Scotland.

These books are available at your local bookstore or wherever books are sold.